Jewish Law

and

Identity

Hermit Kingdom Studies in Christianity and Judaism 2

Jewish Law and Identity

Academic Essays

Heerak Christian Kim

The Hermit Kingdom Press
Cheltenham ♦ Seoul ♦ Bangalore ♦ Cebu

JEWISH LAW AND IDENTITY: ACADEMIC ESSAYS

Copyright © 2005 by Heerak Christian Kim

All rights reserved. No part of this book may be reproduced in any form or by any means, electronic or mechanical, including photocopying, recording, or by any information storage and retrieval system (including computer files in any form), without permission in writing from the publisher.

Hardcover: ISBN 1-59689-046-0
Paperback: ISBN 1-59689-047-9
E-Book: ISBN 1-59689-048-7

Write-To Address:
The Hermit Kingdom Press
3741 Walnut Street, Suite 407
Philadelphia, PA 19104
United States of America

Library of Congress Cataloging-in-Publication Data

Kim, H. C. (Heerak Christian)
 Jewish law and identity : academic essays / Heerak Christian Kim.-- 1st ed.
   p. cm. -- (Hermit kingdom studies in Christianity and Judaism ; 2)
 Includes bibliographical references.
 ISBN 1-59689-046-0 (hardcover : alk. paper) -- ISBN 1-59689-047-9 (pbk. : alk. paper)
 1. Jewish law. 2. Jews--Identity. 3. Bible. O.T.--Criticism, interpretation, etc. I. Title. II. Series.
 BM520.3.K48 2005
 296.1'8--dc22
                          2005019896

For my father and mother

"A classic is a book
that doesn't have to be written again."

W. E. B. Du Bois

Contents

The Abrahamic Covenant and the English Common Law: A Comparative Study in Contract Law to Elucidate the Ancient Israelite Society
⇒ 1 ⇐

Understanding Jewish Law and the Socio-Cultural History of the Jews in the Talmudic Era (70-500 AD)
⇒ 17 ⇐

Midrash and Method: An Examination of the Most Recent Monographs on Methodology
⇒ 52 ⇐

The Servitude-Exodus Narrative and the Passover as a Factual Legend: A Study of Genre and a Formulation of a Historical Criteria
⇒ 76 ⇐

A Window into the Deuteronomistic World: Royal Ideology, Zion Theology, and Social Justice as Texts in Judges 19-21
⇒ 95 ⇐

A Critical and Theoretical Conceptualization of Ritual Studies and Its Application in the Ancient Roman World
⇒ 130 ⇐

Prophecy, Biblical Interpreters,
and the Book of Chronicles
࿐ 157 ࿐

Food, Eating Practices, and Empowerment
in the Narratives of Acts
࿐ 183 ࿐

The Key Signifier of 'Forever'
in Psalms of Solomon 11
࿐ 211 ࿐

Preface

This book contains nine academic papers focusing on Jewish law and identity from various angles. The academic essays in this volume represent research conducted at Harvard University, Brown University, and Cambridge University and exhibit a distinct stamp of the depth of doctoral level training I received at the Hebrew University of Jerusalem (1993-4, 1995-7), where I held the Lady Davis Fellowship, among other international fellowships.

I would like to thank all those who have been supportive of my research at these institutions. I would particularly like to thank the Dorot Foundation, which generously supported my research and provided a travel grant to research in Israel in the summer of 1999.

During the period represented by the essays in the book, I had the pleasure of participating in specialized seminars, which greatly enhanced my research. I would like to mention them in gratitude.

The 8th Jerusalem Summer School in Jewish Studies, sponsored by The Institute for Advanced Studies in Givat Ram, Jerusalem in Israel focused on "Jewish Learning." I would like to thank Professor Daniel Schwartz, the Director, for accepting me into the 1998 seminar comprised of advanced doctoral students and professors around the world.

I had the pleasure of going to Jerusalem again in 1999 to attend the 9th Jerusalem Summer School in Jewish Studies, sponsored by The Institute for Advanced Studies in Israel. The theme was "Jewish Messianism." I would like to thank the director, Professor Isaiah Gafni of the Hebrew University of Jerusalem for accepting me into the seminar and for giving me a fellowship to cover the cost of the program.

I would like to thank the American Academy for Jewish Research for selecting me to be one of the elite members of doctoral researchers to attend its Graduate Research Seminar at the Hebrew Union College – Jewish Institute of Religion in Cincinnati, Ohio, in the summer of 1999. I was the only non-Jew in the seminar, but the participants made me feel very welcome and I thank all of them for their kindness.

I am grateful for the many wonderful opportunities that I have had to challenge my thinking and improve on my research.

I am currently in the process of completing my Ph.D. thesis at Cambridge University in England. I look forward to continuing to share the fruits of my research in further publications in the future. I feel that that is the best way to repay the immense debt of intellectual encouragement and training that I received from some of the greatest minds in the field in this century.

Of course, it would be impossible to conduct research and produce intellectual creation, if it were not for support of kind and loving people. I would like to thank all of you who made an impact in my life. In particular, I would like to thank my father and mother who have always been there for me, through the good times and the bad. So, it is to them that I dedicate this book.

Jewish Law and Identity

The Abrahamic Covenant and the English Common Law: A Comparative Study in Contract Law to Elucidate the Ancient Israelite Society[1]

The Covenant is an important legal concept in the Old Testament. It was a form of contract law seen to bind God in a contractual obligation to the person with whom the contract is made. However, benefits (and liability) came to include a Third Party. In the case of Abraham, the Third Party included his descendants. I would like to illustrate the legal implication of the idea of Third Party obligations in the case of the Abrahamic covenant by examining it in comparison to English contract law, relating to Third Party obligations. Representative English law to be examined is the law of privity of contract. Examining the underlying philosophy behind the concept of privity of contract will help to elucidate the concept of Third Party obligations and its philosophical underpinnings in the Abrahamic Covenant itself as recorded in Genesis. My examination is along the lines of previous comparisons

---

[1] This paper was delivered at the annual conference of the Australian and New Zealand Association of
Theological Schools (ANZATS) and Australian and New Zealand Society for Theological Studies (ANZSTS), held at the University of Western Australia in Perth, Australia (July 4-8, 2005). The research for this paper was conducted primarily in the Cambridge University Law Faculty library (Squire Law Library) and represents a culmination of two-year research into English Common Law with attention to its comparative study value for Jewish Law.

between legal doctuments – such as between Hittite treaties and the covenant of ancient Israel.[2] This paper is presented with the understanding that comparative study of ancient Israelite law in its context and modern law in the context of comparative legal history will elucidate not only the understanding of elements in the law examined, but also the larger cultural context to which the law is presented.

The Abrahamic Covenant as found in Genesis 17 is an important legal document and sheds light on ancient Israelite contract law. The contract law was made between God and Abraham. There are obligations on God's part and also on Abraham's part.[3] Both parties are bound in contract to fulfil necessary

---

[2] Nahum M. Sarna writes: "Turning from the ritualistic to the literary-juristic features of the covenant, an interesting comparative study is now possible. From the Hittite empire records of treaties have survived which regulated relationships between the great kings and their inferior vassals. The documents usually contain a preamble identifying the author of the pact, after which follows a historical prologue describing the past relationships between the contracting parties. Then come the treaty stipulations, the obligations which the superior imposes upon the inferior. A close analysis of God's covenant with Abraham reveals that scripture has here followed a similar legal pattern" (Nahum M. Sarna, *Understanding Genesis* <New York: McGraw-Hill Book Company, 1966>, pp. 126-127). See also, G. E. Mendelhall, "Covenant Forms in Israelite Tradition," *Biblical Archaeologist* 17 (1954), pp. 50-76.

[3] Paul R. Williamson writes that Genesis 17 refers to "a covenant between God and Abraham which is plainly bilateral, involving not only divine promises but also human obligations" (Paul R. Williamson, *Abraham, Israel and the Nations: The Patriarchal Promise and its Covenantal Development in Genesis* <Sheffield: Sheffield Academic Press, 2000>, p. 150).

obligations. Breaking of the contract law on the part of one party releases the other party from contractual obligations. What is particularly interesting in the case of the Abrahamic covenant is that Third Party obligation is built into the contract law. The contract law is between Abraham and God; however, Abraham's descendants as the Third Party are obligated to the contract law made between Abraham and God. The Abrahamic Covenant is a good picture into how Third Party obligations worked in ancient Israelite law.

Comparing the nature of Third Party obligations in the Abrahamic Covenant and English contract law will further elucidate the nature of ancient Israelite contract law principles. I will begin this comparative contract law study by examining the nature of Third Party obligations in ancient Israelite law in greater detail.

In the Abrahamic Covenant in Genesis 17, the contractual obligations of God can be seen as the following: (1) God will make Abraham a father of many nations (vv. 5-6); (2) God will be Abraham's God and the God of Abraham's descendants (v. 7); (3) God will give Canaan to Abraham and his descendants (v. 8). God is obliged to his contractual obligations insofar as Abraham keeps his contractual obligation.[4] Abraham's contractual obligations are (1)

---

[4] John Goldingay writes regarding Genesis 17: "It speaks of descendants and land (17:2-8), but the key-word 'blessing' is replaced by the key-word 'covenant' – which in effect means 'a commitment to bless' (John Goldingay, "The Patriarchs in Scripture and History" in *Essays on the Patriarchal Narratives*, eds. A. R. Millard and D. J. Wiseman <Winona Lake: Eisenbrauns, 1983, pp. 1-34>, p. 5). Goldingay's point reiterates the

to have God as his God (v. 7); (2) to be circumcised and to force circumcision[5] on all who belong to his household, both those being born into his house or bought with money, such as foreign slaves (vv. 11-13); (3) to expel[6] any in his household who refuses circumcision for whatever reason (v. 14). The Abrahamic Covenant represented ancient Israelite contract law binding two parties to their set of obligations. Either side breaking their contractual obligation nulls the requirement of the other party to contract obligations.

The Abrahamic Covenant can be seen as somewhat typical of contract laws in general where two parties are involved in mutual obligations. However, what distinguishes the Abrahamic Covenant is its incorporation of Third Party obligations.

The Third Party in the Abrahamic Covenant can be identified as Abraham's descendants. It is important to note that the Third Party is not present in the "signing" of the contract. Only God and Abraham are present at the time of contractual agreement. However, the contract preserved in the Abrahamic

---

fact of bi-lateral contract on which God's commitment is contingent.

[5] Nahum M. Sarna writes regarding the circumcision directive in Genesis 17: "It has been transferred from the area of formality to the realm of law. Secondly, it cannot be abrogated" (Nahum M. Sarna, *Understanding Genesis* <New York: McGraw-Hill Book Company, 1966>, p. 132). In other words, contract law now obligated circumcision as a legal requirement.

[6] John Skinner notes that "being cut off from his people" can mean excommunication or the death penalty (John Skinner, *A Critical and Exegetical Commentary on Genesis* <Edinburgh: T. & T. Clark, 1930>, p. 294).

Covenant imposes obligations on the Third Party, the descendants of Abraham. The contractual obligation extending to the Third Party is explicitly stated: "As for you, you must keep my covenant, you and your descendants after you for the generations to come" (Genesis 17:9). Paul R. Williamson describes the vicarious role of the Third Party in the contract of the Abrahamic Covenant in this way: "Abraham's covenant status is being transmitted to his זרע."[7]

We see that the contractual obligation required of Abraham is extended to the Third Party which is not present (or even born) at the time of the making of the contract. The Third Party is obligated in all three stipulations demanded of Abraham: (1) they are to have God as their God (v. 7); (2) they are to be circumcised[8] and force circumcision on those who belong to their household or those bought with money, such as foreign slaves (v. 12); (3) they must expel any in their household who refuses circumcision for whatever reason (v. 14). The first two stipulations explicitly mention the Third Party, Abraham's descendants: (1) "to be your God and the God of your descendants after you" (v. 7); (2) "for the generations to come every male among you" (v. 12). The third stipulation implicitly obligates the Third Party. Although Abraham's descendants are not explicitly mentioned in the command to expel the uncircumcised, it is important to note that neither is

---

[7] Williamson, *Abraham, Israel and the Nations*, p. 171.
[8] Paul R. Williamson writes that circumcision served "as a mnemonic device" for Israelites to remember the Abrahamic Covenant and maintain it (Williamson, *Abraham, Israel and the Nations*, p. 185).

Abraham explicitly mentioned. Both Abraham and the Third Party – Abraham's descendants – are implicitly understood to be obligated. This can be definitively inferred in light of the second stipulation which demands circumcision, where Abraham and his descendants are explicitly mentioned. Therefore, the contractual requirement to expel the uncircumcised can be seen as integrally linked to contractual obligation to circumcise. In fact, they are different sides of the same coin.

It is clear that in the Abrahamic Covenant, contractual obligation for Abraham is extended to the Third Party, Abraham's descendants. In fact, the Third Party is bound to the contractual agreement in an integrated (or even vicarious) way. In other words, the stipulations extended to Abraham are equally extended to the Third Party, the descendants of Abraham. Thus, even if Abraham is perfect in his keeping of his contractual obligations,[9] if the non-present Third Party bound to the contract breaks any of the stipulations of the contract, it releases God's contractual obligations. Thus, God is not required to (1) make Abraham a father of many nations;[10] (2) be

---

[9] Thomas L. Thompson describes Abraham as "the wandering, faithful servant of Yahweh, and he wanders not only from Shechem to Bethel and Ai, to Hebron, Gerar, and Beersheba, but even more significantly he wanders from story to story" (Thomas L. Thompson, *The Origin Tradition of Ancient Israel: The Literary Formation of Genesis and Exodus 1-23* <Sheffield: Sheffield Academic Press, 1987>, p. 159). Indeed, the Patriarchal Narratives describe Abraham as obedient to God – as a covenant-keeper.

[10] Paul R. Williamson notes: "If, as is apparently the case, the promise of international expansion is to find its fulfilment

the God of Abraham and the God of Abraham's descendants; (3) give land of Canaan to Abraham and his descendants if Abraham (the other party in the contract) or his descendants (the Third Party) break any of the contractual stipulations for Abraham (integrally extended to the Third Party).

In fact, it is important to note that the contractual stipulations of God are tied to the integrated reality of Abraham's contractual obligations in the Third Party, Abraham's descendants. For instance, although God may continue to observe the first contractual obligation of making Abraham the father of many nations during Abraham's time, if

---

exclusively through the promised line of Isaac, a literal fulfilment (in the sense of physical nations) is ruled out: the Israelites (described from Jacob) and the Edomites (descended from Esau) hardly constituted a "המון גוים" (Williamson, *Abraham, Israel and the Nations*, p. 106). Although Williamson recognizes that God's covenantal obligation to make Abraham the father of many nations is not kept, he prefers to argue that it was fulfilled metaphorically. But why should Williamson assume that God wanted to keep his obligation to make Abraham into the father of many nations? It is reasonable to explore the possibility that God intentionally refused to make Abraham into the father of many nations. It is reasonable to explore the possibility that God intentionally refused to make Abraham the father of many nations because Abraham's descendants (the Third Party) broke the covenantal obligation to Abraham, which was extended to them. Thus, the breaking of the contract by the Third Party made Abraham liable in the vicarious role of the Third Party in ancient Israelite contract law. Because Abraham's part of the covenant was broken (by the Third Party representing him), God chose not to keep his obligation to make Abraham the father of many nations. In other words, the violations of the Third Party released God from his contractual obligations to Abraham.

Abraham's descendants break any of the contractual stipulations demanded of Abraham and by extension to the Third Party, then God is not obligated to fulfil his stipulation. The end result is that, in fact, Abraham would not be the father of many nations if Abraham's descendants break any of the contractual stipulations.

This principle applies to other two contractual stipulations of God. For instance, the second contractual stipulation for God that he will be Abraham's God and the God of Abraham's descendants can be broken by God if the Third Party violates the contractual stipulation required of Abraham, to which they are tied.

This is the same with the third stipulation that God will give the land of Canaan to Abraham and his descendants. God can break his contractual obligation if Abraham's descendants break any of the stipulations of the contract (even if Abraham perfectly keeps them).

In a sense, therefore, the benefits of the covenant which was to continue after Abraham's death will stop if the Third Party (Abraham's descendants) breaks any of the contractual stipulation to which Abraham was bound.

What does this say about ancient Israelite contract law? The Third Party plays an integral role in contract law. Even a non-existent or a theoretical Third Party is bound to the contract in a vicarious way. Thus, a Third Party can be attached to one of the contractual parties as an integral part of it. The Third Party is liable to the contract and becomes the beneficiary of the contract although they were not present (and even non-existent) at the time of the contract making. The end result is that if the Third Party violates the contract, it is as if the party which it represents has violated the contract. The original terms of the contract can become null and void. Thus, the other party – in this case, God – is no longer obligated to keep his part of the contract.[11]

The integral role that the Third Party plays in ancient Israelite law is distinctive and elucidates some things about ancient Israelite society. First of all, the Third Party principle explains the power of substitution or vicarious role. It is as if the Third Party becomes one of the parties of the original contract.

This is quite different in ethos from the nature of contract law in other societies. The case of English common law will elucidate the difference. In particular, the legal principle of privity of contracts will be greatly enlightening.

English contract law is clear in excluding the Third Party from the contract. Only the two parties engaging in the contract are bound by the contract. In other words, only the two parties engaged in the contract-making are bound in the liability as well as the benefits of the contract. The Third Party is not liable for breaking the contract made by two parties in the bilateral contract. And the Third Party cannot claim benefits on the contract made by the two contracting parties. This legal concept in English

---

[11] This can be seen as a type of retroactive annulment of the contract as the result of the violations by the Third Party even if the actual party of the contract was completely faithful to the contract.

common law is called privity. In fact, it would be accurate to say that the exclusion of the Third Party from the contract is a foundational principle in English contract law. A. G. Guest describes the important principle of English contract law:

> We come now to deal with the effects of a valid contract when formed, and to ask, To whom does the obligation extend? What are the limits of a contractual agreement? This question must be considered under two separate headings: (1) the imposition of liabilities upon a third party, and (2) the acquisition of rights by a third party. We shall see that the general rule of the common law is that no one but the parties to a contract can be bound by it, or entitled under it. This principle is known as that of *privity of contract*.[12]

And privity of contract is a rule that dominates and governs English contract law in regards to Third Party benefits and liabilities.

Several important legal cases affirmed the English common law principle of privity of contract. *Tweddle v. Atkinson* (1861)[13] concluded that even if

---

[12] A. G. Guest, *Anson's Law of Contract* (Oxford: Clarendon Press, 1975), p. 395.
[13] The plaintiff was to marry the defendant's daughter. The defendant (B) promised plaintiff's father (A) to pay the plaintiff (C) a marriage dowry. Thus, the plaintiff was the Third Party in

the two contracting parties (A and B) explicitly agree that the Third Party (C) can sue B on the contract between A and B, the general rule of English Common Law prohibits it.[14] In other words, a valid contract under English contract law cannot include any clause regarding the Third Party; it is simply not enforceable under English Common Law.

The denial of fundamental contractual right of the Third Party was reiterated in *Dunlop Pneumatic Tyre Co., Ltd. v. Selfridge & Co., Ltd.* (1915). Lord Haldane stated the English Court's official stance: "In the law of England certain principles are fundamental. One is that only a person who is a party to a contract can sue on it. Our law knows nothing of a *ius quaesitum tertio* arising by way of contract."[15] Thus, Lord Haldane encapsulated the essence of English contract law. English contract law limits the liability and the benefit to the two parties making the contract. The Third Party is excluded.

The English Common Law principle of privity of contract was again upheld in a major contract law case of *Beswick v. Beswick* (1968). Particularly significant in this case is the claim by Lord Denning against the law of privity. Lord Denning said that it was "at bottom ... only a rule of

---

the contract. It was upheld that the plaintiff (the Third Party) could not enforce the agreement between the contracting parties (A and B). Thus, in effect the contract entered into by A and B on behalf of C was by the standards of English contract law null and void.

[14] Aubrey L. Diamond, W. R. Cornish, A. S. Grabiner, and R. S. Nock, *Sutton and Shannon on Contracts* (London: Butterworths, 1970), pp. 76-77.

[15] Guest, *Anson's Law of Contract*, p. 404.

procedure"[16] and it could be overcome by the Third Party joining the promise (one of the two parties making the contract) as a party to the contractual agreement.[17] G. H. Treitel notes that Lord Denning's view is a minority view and all the speeches in the House of Lords "assume the correctness of the commonly accepted view that a contract can only be enforced by the parties to it."[18] A. G. Guest agrees and states that the House of Lords "proceeded on the assumption ... that no stranger can sue on a contract even if made for his benefit."[19] A. W. B. Simpson also concurs and notes *Beswick v. Beswick* (1968) as a modern example of the fundamental doctrine of privity of contract determining contract cases.[20]

It is clear that foundational to English contract law is the principle of privity of contract. The contract is between two parties making the agreement. A

---

[16] Guest, *Anson's Law of Contract*, p. 405.

[17] It can appear on the surface that this procedure would make English contract law similar to ancient Israelite contract law. But there are key differences. In *Beswick v. Beswick* (1968), the uncle's wife (C) was alive at the time of the uncle (A) making the contract with his nephew (B), whereas in the case of Abrahamic covenant the descendants of Abraham were not even born. More importantly, in the Abrahamic covenant, the benefits (as well as the obligations) were the same for Abraham (A) and Abraham's descendants (C). There was a vicarious relationship. This would certainly not be the case even following Lord Denning's stance.

[18] G. H. Treitel, *Law of Contract* (London: Stevens & Sons, 1975), p. 422.

[19] Guest, *Anson's Law of Contract*, p. 405.

[20] A. W. B. Simpson, *A History of the Common Law of Contract: The Rise of the Action of Assumpsit* (Oxford: Clarendon Press, 1975), p. 475.

Third Party, even explicitly mentioned in the contract, is excluded from the contract – its benefits as well as its liabilities. This fundamental principle of English contract law differs completely with the principle of contract law in ancient Israel. The Third Party certainly can be tied to the contract in its benefits and liabilities. Furthermore, the Third Party can have a vicarious relationship with one of the two parties making a contract. This is the case even when the Third Party is not in existence (or even born). This is the case in the contract made between God and Abraham as recorded in Genesis 17. Although the two parties actually making the contract were God and Abraham, Abraham's descendants (who were not even born) were bound to the contract integrally as the Third Party. In the case of ancient Israelite contract law, the Third Party (Abraham's descendants) was integrally bound in a vicarious way to one of the two parties (Abraham) who actually made the contract. Thus, ancient Israelite contract law fundamentally differs from English contract law and its philosophical outlook and premise. This fundamental difference in the relationship of the Third Party to a contract in the case of the ancient Israelite contract law of the Abrahamic Covenant is a key that opens the door to understanding of contract law in ancient Israelite society and, by extension, its philosophical outlook and premise.

It is easy to see how the difference highlighted by comparing English Common Law and ancient Israelite law in the area of contract law adds to our understanding of ancient Israelite law and the ancient Israelite society. The reality of the vicarious, integrated role of the Third Party in the ancient Israelite contract of the Abrahamic Covenant as highlighted in my study opens the door to understanding the nature and the function of ancient Israelite contract law and, by extension, ancient Israelite society. Certainly, more work in the area of ancient Israelite contact law can be done building on my study on the Third Party principle in ancient Israelite law. I hope that many will be encouraged to pursue this study as the result of my paper delivered at ANZATS/ANZSTS conference in Perth, Australia. I, for one, am excited about engaging in further research on ancient Israelite law, building on this examination.

Bibliography

Christiansen, Ellen Juhl. *The Covenant in Judaism and Paul: A Study of Ritual Boundaries as Identity Markers.* Leiden: E. J. Brill, 1995.

Diamond, Aubrey L., W. R. Cornish, A. S. Grabiner, and R. S. Nock. *Sutton and Shannon on Contracts.* London: Butterworths, 1970.

Firmage, Edwin B., Bernard G. Weiss, and John W. Welch (Editors). *Religion and Law: Biblical-Judaic and Islamic Perspectives.* Winona Lake: Eisenbrauns, 1990.

Guest, A. G. *Anson's Law of Contract.* Oxford: Clarendon Press, 1975.

Mendelhall, G. E. "Covenant Forms in Israelite Tradition." *Biblical Archaeologist* 17 (1954), pp. 50-76.

Millard, A. R., and D. J. Wiseman. *Essays on the Patriarchal Narratives.* Winona Lake: Eisenbrauns, 1983.

Rendsburg, Gary A. *The Redaction of Genesis.* Winona Lake: Eisenbrauns, 1986.

Sarna, Nahum M. *Understanding Genesis.* New York: McGraw-Hill Book Company, 1966.

Simpson, A. W. B. *A History of the Common Law of Contract: The Rise of the Action of Assumpsit.* Oxford: Clarendon Press, 1975.

Skinner, John. *A Critical and Exegetical Commentary on Genesis.* Edinburgh: T. & T. Clark, 1930.

Thompson, Thomas L. *The Origin Tradition of Ancient Israel: The Literary Formation of Genesis and Exodus 1-23.* Sheffield: Sheffield Academic Press, 1987.

Treitel, G. H. *The Law of Contract.* London: Stevens & Sons, 1975.

Von Rad, Gerhard. *Genesis: A Commentary.* Translated by John H. Marks. London: SCM Press Ltd., 1961.

Weinfeld, Moshe. *The Promise of the Land: The Inheritance of the Land of Canaan by the Israelites.* Berkeley: University of California Press, 1993.

Williamson, Paul R. *Abraham, Israel and the Nations: The Patriarchal Promise and Its Covenantal Development in Genesis.* Sheffield: Sheffield Academic Press, 2000.

Understanding Jewish Law and the Socio-Cultural History of the Jews in the Talmudic Era (70-500 AD)[1]

If you were to undertake the writing of a history of the Yavne period (70-132 AD) in Jewish history, what steps would you take and what pitfalls would you try to avoid in the gathering and organization of the source material for your work?

If I were to undertake the writing of a history of the Yavne period, I would take the steps of gathering synchronic and diachronic data. The pitfalls I would try to avoid in the gathering and organization of the source material for my work are uncritical examination of the sources, on the one hand, and a flippant dismissal of them, on the other hand. After critical examination of the gathered data, I will find steps to correlate them into a coherent history writing.

---

[1] By special arrangement, my Brown University Ph.D. program in Judaic Studies included 50% doctoral course work from Harvard University and 50% doctoral course work from Brown University. In this context, I participated in a doctoral seminar in Jewish Studies at Harvard University in 1999, taught by Professsor Isaiah Gafni, who was a visiting professor from the Hebrew University of Jerusalem in Israel. I would like to thank him for his wonderful guidance. Among fellow researchers in the doctoral seminar, I would like to thank Elisheva Septimus from Harvard University for her insights. This study in Talmudic law and society is represented in the question – answer format.

I would first like to elaborate on the initial essential step of gathering data. To compose an effective history of the Yavne period, it is important to gather the necessary synchronic and diachronic data. Synchronic data is important for providing immediate context and also comparative basis for the construction of the history of the period. Much of the synchronic data will be found in ancient Roman history, particularly Late Antiquity. In this regard, it will be important to examine primary source material from the Yavne period as well as secondary ancient sources that describe that period.

The use of ancient Roman sources implicitly recognizes the necessity of the larger context for comprehension of a particular history. It is important to separate the primary sources composed during the Yavne period and secondary sources from Late Antiquity that describe the Yavne period. The primary source will include the contemporary eye-witness accounts as well as writings about the past. Implicit in the examination of the latter is the understanding that such writings most likely also reflect contemporary concerns as well.

To provide an example of this, it would be beneficial to examine the literature during the time of Emperor Augustus. As a patron, Augustus commissioned such leading literary figures as Virgil and Horace to write literature that essentially praised his rule and his Pax Romana. Often, the literary glorification was not direct, but rather couched within an epic story or a description of the past, such as *Aeniad*, which glorified classical Roman virtues. Besides being propaganda for Augustus, the literature of the

Golden Age also functioned as a propaganda for his moralist legislation, such as *lex Papia Poppaea*. In this tradition of describing the past reflecting the concerns of the present, one can view ancient Roman sources from the Yavnean period, writing about the past. The example from Virgil further reflects the diversity of literature that could be used as a source for synchronic data. Synchronic data is important because nothing happens in isolation from its context. And a history of the Yavne period had as its context ancient Roman Empire.

Other synchronic data can be utilized as well that are more particular in nature. By particular, I refer to sources that might have belonged to a limited number of people or was of concern to a small group within the ancient Roman Empire. This data will provide primarily comparative information rather than general contextual information. The comparison can be examined in regards to influence (in either direction), but by in large this kind of comparative study is helpful in showing common shared trends of the period. In this regard, Christian documents will prove helpful.

Much of the Christian texts that came to be included in the Christian canon received their final redaction in the Yavnean period, thereby somewhat reflecting the concerns of the Yavnean period. Also, there are other non-canonical early Christian documents, such as *Didache*, which some scholars attribute to the Yavnean period. Just as the above synchronic treatment of the ancient Roman sources must first be treated in its own right, these early Christian documents dated to the Yavnean period must receive attention on their own right. These individual treatments of the synchronic data will later be combined with the diachronic treatment to provide a history of the Yavne period. Diachronic data is also important for the writing of a history of the Yavne period in Jewish history. Particularly important in this regard is diachronic data from Jewish history. For instance, literature from pre-Yavne period will be examined, particularly sources from the late Second Temple period. Collectively, Jewish writers such as Philo and Josephus, Qumran documents, and other "sectarian" documents of the period, often referred to as "pseudepigrapha," will provide a good basis on which to make some conclusions about the Yavnean period.

Philo has often been portrayed as a hellenized Jew representing Hellenistic Judaism in Alexandria. Some have, therefore, previously questioned his relevance for studying Judaism in the Land of Israel. In his article, "The Modern Study of Ancient Judaism,"[2] Shaye Cohen questions such previous premise and points to the need to recognize the coherence of hellenistic influence for both Jews in the Diaspora as well as for those in the Land of Israel. Cohen writes:

> There is now wide agreement that the terms 'Hellenistic Judaism' and 'Palestinian Judaism' are not antonyms. Valid distinctions can be drawn

---

[2]S. J. D. Cohen, "The Modern Study of Ancient Judaism" *in The State of Jewish Studies*, eds. S. J. D. Cohen and E. L. Greenstein (Detroit: Wayne State University Press, 1990), pp. 55-79.

> between the Greek-speaking Judaisms of the diaspora and the Greek-, Hebrew- or Aramaic-speaking Judaisms of the Land of Israel, but all the Jews of Greco-Roman antiquity, no matter what language they spoke or where they lived, were 'hellenized' to some degree" (p. 58).

In this light, not only will Philo's writings provide information of Jews in Alexandria or in the Diaspora, it could also shed light on the Yavnean history itself.

Besides Philo, Josephus can also provide diachronic data for the writing of the Yavnean history. In fact, Josephus did most of his writing in the Yavnean period as a court historian in Rome. Josephus wrote predominantly of the past, but his writings most likely reflect his concerns as well as concerns of his contemporaneous Jews. One problem facing him is the question regarding the extent of his connectedness to the Jewish community in Yavne after the destruction of the Temple in 70 AD. However, his sources are crucial for providing information regarding the pre-Yavnean environment in the Land of Israel and the corresponding Jewish experience. Thus, Josephus can be treated as a pre-Yavnean source, as well as a possible Yavnean source.

In addition to Philo and Josephus, Qumran documents further provide diachronic data. Harmut Stegemann has dated some of the Dead Sea scrolls originally to the fourth or fifth century BC, partly based on his perception of the ideology contained in these documents. However, scholarly consensus is that the Dead Sea scrolls are dated from late third century BC to about first century AD. Much of the documents recovered from Qumran, therefore, would provide essential diachronic data for the Yavnean period.

Recent developments in Qumran studies which perceives recovered documents as not *necessarily* "sectarian" in nature, but rather shared by the larger Jewish audience, would provide a picture into the importance of the Dead Sea scrolls for the writing of the history of the Yavnean period. Since the study of Qumran documents in academia is in its nascent stages, it makes utilization of Qumran documents a little bit difficult. To further complicate matters, Qumran studies have often been conducted in isolation, so that there is growing preponderance of scholarly works on theology or literary structure, but not much works of historical nature based on these ancient texts. This is not surprising in light of the isolationist tendency in Qumran studies.

No substantial work of history can be written by using works that is often non-historical in nature and when it is isolated from its context. Eileen Schuller has called for an integrated study of the Dead Sea scrolls. In her article, "Prayer, Hymnic, and Liturgical Texts" in *The Community of the Renewed Covenant: The Notre Dame Symposium on the Dead Sea Scrolls*,[3] which was published in 1994,

---

[3] Eugene Ulrich and James Vanderkam (eds.), *The Community of the Renewed Covenant: The Notre Dame Symposium on the Dead Sea Scrolls* (Notre Dame: University of Notre Dame Press, 1994).

Schuller writes: "I am increasingly convinced that real progress will be made in the next years only if Qumran scholarship now becomes less isolated and more cognizant of and involved in other related disciplines" (p. 171). With real progress in integrated study of the Dead Sea scrolls will come invaluable source for the construction of Yavnean history.

Besides Philo, Josephus, Qumran documents, other "sectarian" writings must be examined as well. These include the Apocrypha and works that have been referred to as "Pseudepigrapha." These works have been dated from the middle of the second Temple period and some even into the Rabbinic period. There have been more integrated studies of individual documents in this corpus than of Qumran documents. Thus, these documents provide needed internal contextual studies in the construction of the Yavnean history.

This is not to say that there are not problems within this corpus of sources. For example, one of the problem facing scholars is that of identification of a document as originally Jewish or Christian. To complicate matters, some scholars argue for an essential Jewish nature of the document with Christian interpolations in later transmissional stage. However, the problem of identification of a document as essentially Christian or Jewish and the development of that identification as a major exercise in scholarship indicate the relative proximity of criterion for determining the document as Christian or Jewish. In fact, this might not be surprising if one takes the claim of James Dunn seriously. Dunn argues that the separation between Christians and

Jews did not happen before 135 AD. He argues that Christian Jews participated in Jewish activities and Jews did not necessarily ostracize Christian Jews from participation in those activities. With the failed messianic expectation of the Bar Kokhba revolt came pointed suspicion of messianic-centric Jewish movements.

Scholarship regarding the separation between Jews and Christians was initiated fairly recently in the wake of the claim by Geza Vermes that Jesus was a Jew and, therefore, needs to be studied in that context. In the larger framework of scholarly inquiry, this can be seen as a logical procession of "the new quest for the historical Jesus" that Bultmann's students, like Conzelmann, started several decades ago in Germany, in which scholars came to appreciate the historical context of Jesus and the immediate and integral relevance of Jewish history. This movement saw immediate result in works that started to treat Jewish history in its own right, apart from its direct relevance to Christianity, exhibited in such works as that of Martin Hengel, particularly in his work on the Zealots. Emphasis on context has a tendency to legitimize and encourage study of seemingly separate historical traditions in their own right, since the assumption is that in order to properly understand the context, various factors within that context must be given fair and detailed treatment.

Philo, Josephus, Qumran documents, and other "sectarian writings," indeed, aid in the diachronic study of Jewish history, with a particular attention to the Yavnean period. Perhaps, more useful than these for understanding the Yavnean period in the diachronic study of Jewish history may be the Rabbinic works themselves. For one, Mishnah was codified around 200 AD. Since this is not so much removed from the Yavnean period, one could attribute relative accuracy to the purported events and saying recorded in the document. Therefore, one can argue in light of relative proximity of the events in the Yavnean period, that the collective memory of Jews at the time of the final redaction of Mishnah closely proximated actual events and sayings of sages in the Yavnean period. After all, we are talking about a few decades. Whatever the "agenda" of the final redactors of the Mishnah, they could not have so altered the events and sayings of the sages from the Yavnean period that it conflicted with the collective memory of the audience.

In this light, ancient historian Kurt Raaflaub's research into collective memory in regards to Homer and his literary composition is helpful, but not necessarily binding in the study of the Mishnah. Raaflaub asserts that Homeric documents reflect predominantly (or even exclusively) concerns of the Homeric time and reflects the collective memory of his audience regarding the distantly removed epic past, which was in fact shaped by contemporary concerns. In regards to the Mishnah, there are several points that provide argument for the accuracy of the Mishnaic account. First of all, as mentioned previously, there is a shorter chronological distance of decades, rather than centuries. Also, as Professor Daniel Schwartz of the Hebrew University of Jerusalem indicated in a private conversation in 1993, there were independent notes floating around that were used in the composition/redaction of Rabbinic texts. This contrasts with the purely oral transmissional nature of the Homeric epics. With actual written notes, there is a greater tendency toward faithfulness to the original event and sayings. Thus, fundamental reliability of the Mishnah and other contemporaneous Rabbinic documents, such as the Tosefta, must be recognized. The question, therefore, does not relate to their essential reliability, but rather to the needed methodology for writing a critical history of the Yavnean period.

In regards to other Rabbinic documents that are further removed in time from the Yavnean period, such as the Talmuds and Midrashic works, I would argue that they are still useful for the examination of the Yavnean period. First of all, floating notes, that might have been ignored by the final redactors of the Mishnah, could have been used by compilers of the Talmuds or Midrashic works. Since codification of Mishnah and Tosefta brought about legitimacy of such written compilations, it would not be surprising if the process of compilation of the Talmuds even along with separate notes was immediately in motion shortly after the codification of the Tannaitic documents. Even despite continuous compilation and redaction until its final redaction several centuries after the final redaction of the Mishnah, the Talmuds could have exhibited relative faithfulness to its sources and to actual events and saying of sages.

This argument becomes more convincing in light of the Medieval Torah commentaries and their relationship to Midrash. The commentators were centuries removed from Midrash, but exhibit relative faithfulness to Midrash in much of their interpretation. This is not to say that there was not a certain amount of creativity. In fact, commentaries by Ibn Ezra exhibit high level of creativity and analysis of grammar or Hebrew structure that exhibit his inheritance of the Hebrew philologist tradition, such as that of Hayyuj. This, in fact, can be seen as Ibn Ezra's reflection of the contemporary concerns of the Jewish community in the Middle Ages, in which heretical literalist movement is seen as having, in part, propelled biblical exegesis toward *peshat* and greater grammatical analysis to combat heresy on its own grounds. However, that does not dismiss the fact that wherever Midrashic interpretation is presented, there is a great deal of accuracy to the original Midrashic source.

Thus, Rabbinic documents are particularly crucial for the construction of the history of the Yavnean period. Rabbinic documents form a part of the diachronic data that also includes "pre-Yavnean" works of Philo, Josephus, the Qumran documents, and other "sectarian" writings. This diachronic data must be combined with synchronic data that provides the picture of the larger context of ancient Roman Empire and also other synchronic data from contemporaneous particularistic groups, such as the Christians, which provide important comparative data that shows a picture into the socio-historical reality of the time.

After combining all the synchronic and diachronic data, one can begin writing a coherent history of the Yavnean period that is written from the perspective of a modern historian, utilizing the rules of academic historiography. This is a process of its own. A student of history can choose to focus on different aspects. One could write a work of more traditional historiography which focuses on politics and religion. One could also focus on social history with implementation of sociological and anthropological methodology. One could furthermore engage in creative historiography, such as psycho-history, gender and ethnic studies. With the completion of this process can one actually say that we have a modern academic work of history of the Yavnean period.

"Torah luminaries never took upon themselves to probe the history of the people of Israel"
(R. Hayyim Ozer Grodzinski).

In what respect would you agree with this statement as it relates to the talmudic sages, and where would you take issue?

I would agree with Rabbi Hayyim Ozer Grodzinski's statement that "Torah luminaries never took upon themselves to probe the history of the people of Israel" in that the Talmudic sages did not engage in historiography in the modern sense of the term. However, I would disagree with the above statement in the sense that the Talmudic sages were concerned about the past of the people of Israel. This is reflected in the sheer fact that past tradition is preserved. Not only that, the main source of the past people of Israel, the Tanakh, is used as a crucial source for the Talmudic sages. Furthermore, even the phrase מהי דהוה הוה that may seem to show lack of interest in the past indicates that in the context of the passages in which they are found, they actually are not proof of disregard for the past.

Indeed, the Talmudic sages did not engage in historiography in the modern sense of the word. They did not gather sources and provide a critical, coherent work of history covering a period of time in the past history of Israel. The Talmudic sages preferred to discuss topics and in doing so presented various comments purportedly belonging to previous sages. Thus, the collection provides an anthology of sayings, rather than a critical presentation of the events, or causes and effects, or other presentation that could be seen as historiography.

To illustrate this point, I would like to discuss characterization of the Mishnah by modern scholars. No leading scholar to my knowledge has referred to the Mishnah as a book of history of law, let alone a work of historiography. Epstein has referred to the Mishnah as a law code, and Albeck has referred to it as a text book of law. Implicit in these characterizations is the understanding the Mishnah does not do historiography.

I would like to pose the question regarding the possibility of the characterization of the Mishnah as an oral history of law. Examination of oral history and its application as a distinctive historiographical form are fairly recent phenomena in the conservative field of history, or historiography, which emphasizes written sources. However, creative historical works of Carlo Ginzburg have shown the merits of oral history for understanding the past. It might be beneficial to examine the Mishnah, and the rest of the Rabbinic corpus (including the Talmuds), in light of new advances in oral history as historiography. In this light, serious reassessment of Ephraim E. Urbach's position is warranted. In "Halakha and History,"[4] an article published in 1976, Urbach writes: "The method of halakhic transmission is actually historical and not normative, because it gives not only the prevailing view but also the contradictory one, even if it has been abolished" (p. 118).

It is, however, important to keep in mind that oral history is not the same as oral tradition. The chief difference is that oral history examines historiographic forms and merits for historical inquiry that a (strategic) collection of oral sources, including methods of its transmission (which oral tradition is), has for the modern academic study of history. Thus, this qualifies my position. Although in the current state of theoretical inquiry relating to historiography, I would have to agree that Talmudic sages did not engage in historiography, with advances in theoretical rumination regarding the nature and function of historiography as a phenomena along with advances in the developing inquiry into oral history, I would most likely be willing to revise my position.

---

[4] E. E. Urbach, "Halakha and History" in *Essays in Honour of W. D. Davies*, ed. R. Hammerton-Kelley and R. Scroggs (Leiden: Brill, 1976), pp. 112-128.

However, I would certainly disagree with Rabbi Hayyim Ozer Grodzinski's statement that "Torah luminaries never took upon themselves to probe the history of the people of Israel" in the sense that the Talmudic sages were concerned about the past of the people of Israel. In this, Urbach's statement in "Halakha and History" is significant. There, Urbach writes:

> First of all we must ask ourselves whether the decline in the external production of historical writings means also a decline in the sense of history. We can prove the opposite. The awareness of historical change was a living factor in this period" (p. 115).

Indeed, the primarily proof of concern for the past and awareness of historical change is found in the fact that past tradition is preserved. Statements by previous sages are recorded along with debates of the past. Different and even newer opinions are also introduced. In fact, the Talmudic literature exhibits internal dynamics and differences (and similarity) of opinion over a period of time. This certainly shows concern for the past as well as awareness of historical change.

Of course, statements regarding possible fabrication by the final redactors of the Talmud must be considered in a serious light by the historian. But this does not abrogate the fact that the Talmudic sages were concerned with the past. If they were not, then there would have been no reason to feel the need to refer to sages of the past, even in "fabrication." There is an implicit understanding that the past is significant for the compilers of the Talmud as well as a clear indication that it was important for the audience for whom it was compiled. Why else would Talmud take on the structure that it did?

Not only does past collection of sayings of sages function as a form of oral history collection, thereby showing the concern of the Talmudic sages in the past of the people of Israel, the fact that Tanakh functions as an important source text of the Talmudic sages indicates a concern with the past of the people of Israel. Granted, Tanakh is not used in the same way in Halakhah as in Midrash, but dependence on Tanakh is evident in Talmudic sages. There are many examples of elaboration of biblical laws found in Leviticus and Deuteronomy. This indicates their concern for the past of the history of the people of Israel. Thus, there is an implicit recognition of the relevance of the past for the present and exposition to relate past to the present.

Besides the exposition of Tanakh and the application for contemporary times, Talmudic sages exhibit interest in historical dynamics of the people of Israel, by recognizing the break between the biblical times and their situation. One example of this is found in the Rabbinic perception that prophecy has ceased. In his article, "Concepts of Periodization and Causality in Talmudic Literature,"[5] Isaiah Gafni writes:

---

[5] Isaiah Gafni, "Concepts of Periodization and Causality in Talmudic Literature," *Jewish History* 10 (1996) pp. 21-38.

> One of the major lines of demarcation in rabbinic eyes between the ancient, Biblical past and their contemporary state of existence was the cessation of prophecy. .... For the rabbis, the onset of the Hellenistic period designated the end of prophecy, and this fact is framed in what can be seen as a type of rabbinic periodization..." (p. 32).

This quote brings out a further important point. There was a form of periodization in the Rabbinic mind.

Rabbinic sages exhibit awareness of the ordered past and described it in terms of periodization. Gafni records scholarly assertion that likely due to Zoroastrian influence of division of cosmic history into three stages, Rabbis might have also periodized the world into three distinct stages (pp. 23-24). Furthermore, Rabbinic corpus exhibits political periodization as well, as is the case in *Seder Olam*, in which one finds historical process subdivided into political eras.

However, Gafni notes that these eras are affected not by natural laws and forces but rather by divine element. Thus, Gafni argues that this provides a picture into the Rabbinic perception of irrelevancy of history (p. 26). In this light, one could argue that there is a lack of modern perception of history and historiography where causes are identified in the natural realm. But that does not disavow the fact that the Rabbis engaged in an examination of the past and even attempted to order their past in a systematic form. This definitely shows Rabbinic interest in the past and goes to disprove Rabbi Hayyim Ozer Grodzinski's claim that "Torah luminaries never took upon themselves to probe the history of the people of Israel."

Furthermore, even the phrase מהי דהוה הוה, which appears fifteen times in the Babylonian Talmud and also in the Jerusalem Talmud (Urbach, p. 120; Gafni notes that the phrase appears in fourteen Babylonian Talmud *sugyot* [p. 29]), that has been used to indicate lack of interest by Talmudic sages on the past, shows that in the larger context of the passages in which they are found this phrase does not do that, but rather, it indicates a concern with the past. Urbach writes: "The dictum 'what happened, happened,' which seemingly was intended to militate against preoccupation with the past, is actually employed to stress its importance" (p. 122). And Gafni notes that the phrase is used to indicate *fait accompli* that cannot be undone or a reality in the past that has no real significance for the present (p. 30). Gafni also notes the possibility of the use of the phrase מהי דהוה הוה as a literary device by anonymous Talmudic redactors for cases in which Rabbinic discourse entered unfamiliar ground (pp. 31-32). Thus, it is clear that מהי דהוה הוה was not intended to indicate Rabbinic disdain for the past.

Indeed, the Talmudic sages might not have practiced historiography in the modern sense of the term (at least in the current state of theoretical research on historiography), but they were certainly concerned with the past and probed the history of the people of Israel.

Does this suggested lack of historical interest on the part of the rabbis affect our own uses of the material for the purpose of producing histories of the period? If yes -- in which areas?

The lack of historical, or historiographical, interest on the part of the Rabbis does have an impact on our own uses of the material for the purpose of producing histories of the period primarily in the area of critical source and historical framework. I will elaborate on these two points in the following paragraphs.

By critical source, I am referring to sources that are ready for immediate usage for the construction of a coherent history. Since we have, by in large, a collection of sayings and materials that are preserved without critical assessment as to its usability for construction of a work of historiography in the modern sense of the term, we need to do this exercise ourselves. It is important here to recognize that it was not the concern of the Rabbis to construct such a critical historiography. Thus, since it was not their intent for their literary composition, we cannot blame them for the form which their literary corpus took.

Furthermore, it is important to note that critical examination of sources is required of all sources to some extent; it is not, and should not, be particular to the Rabbinic sources before us. But I do recognize the fact that some sources have undergone critical examination of a sort and would be easier to use as a historical source. There are cases in ancient Roman historiography which examined sources before them and provided information on the contents. In these cases, we have a reference from secondary sources from ancient Rome that provides a reference point for the primary sources from that period.

For instance, *Res Gestae* of Augustus was used by later Roman historian Suetonius in describing the Augustan principate. *Res Gestae* is basically a list of accomplishments that Augustus himself had written down, not dissimilar to the Mesha Inscription from the ancient Near East. What is particularly useful in regards to Suetonius is that his position is somewhat anti-Julio-Claudian dynasty as he favored previous historical sources written by those belonging to the Senatorial class, which was discontent with the Julio-Claudian dynasty for wresting power away from the Roman Senate. Thus, for the modern historian, such internal Roman historiography provides valuable critical sources which can be further used for critical examination according to modern historiography. In regards to the Rabbinic texts, such internal critical historiography is missing. Thus, the modern historian is left with the task of starting from the very beginning in her effort to construct a modern history of the Rabbinic period.

Perhaps somewhat related is the question of historical framework. Since there is no work of history from the ancient world for the Rabbinic period like those of Josephus or Tacitus, the modern historian is left with the question of where to start. What kind of framework should be used in the construction of Rabbinic history? This question becomes acute when one examines modern historiography relating to the late Second Temple period or Late Antiquity. Often, Josephus and Tacitus provide the basic framework around which the modern historian can reconstruct her history. The modern historian can choose to deviate from that essential framework, but the fact remains that the Josephan framework or Tacitian framework was the foundation on which such critical decision was made. Thus, it is not surprising that many modern historians actually devote monographs to an ancient historian, as was the case with Shaye Cohen and his *Josephus in Galilee and Rome* and Sir Ronald Syme and his monograph on Tacitus. Examination of a representative ancient historian provides not only a picture into ancient history but also an essential historiographical framework for the modern historian in her search for "Was wirklich gewesen ist." For the Rabbinic period, we have no such historiographical writing on which to build. The primary historiographical framework needs to be constructed from fragmentary sources.

This, indeed, is a monumental task, perhaps requiring an academic school dedicated to such a process over a long period of time. The project could be likened to the Chicago School of Religious Studies. University of Chicago under the leadership of such scholarly figures like Mircea Eliade shifted and guided the way of asking questions regarding religion that has produced tomes of literature on the Sacred and the Profane. It created a new academic discourse and a frame of reference. Eliade's students began to fill in the gaps and strengthen his theories.

Such individuals and Kees Bolle have carried on Eliade's endeavor in phenomenological inquiry of religion. Another similar example would be Cyrus Gordon and his effort to shift Hebrew Studies with Ugaritic as the primary reference point and not Arabic. In his effort, he has opened a new framework for asking questions about Biblical Hebrew and the history of ancient Israelites. Although hundreds of years of Arabic-centered Hebrew linguistics, going all the way back to ben Janah and Hayyuj, have proved to be the framework that could not be supplanted, Cyrus Gordon's contribution to Hebrew philology shows its staying power in the integral necessity for discussion of Ugaritic in Hebrew philology. Gordon's students have carried on his vision for an integrated study of Hebrew philology with a primary ancient Near Eastern focus and a secondary Aegean reference. This is evident in the growing interest on the interrelation between ancient Semitic philology and classical philology and the cultures that produced them.

Framework producing character of Eliade's Chicago School of Religious Studies and Gordon's Near Eastern Studies stand as a child's play next to the efforts to produce Rabbinic history. That does not mean that it cannot be done. But in the current trend of deconstructionist examination of Rabbinic sources propelled by Jacob Neusner's literary criticism, historical construction stands as a difficult exercise. Neusner's deconstructionist efforts have found progression in that direction as is evident in his "top student" William S. Green. Whereas Neusner argues that ideas and sayings can be attributed to various Rabbinic Schools, Green argues that this cannot be done. This conclusion is not surprising in light of the deconstructionist academic discourse framework that Neusner has created. This is not to dismiss Neusner's contribution to the critical study of Rabbinic sources, which has been given credit by non-deconstructionist scholars, like Shaye Cohen. However, making deconstruction a primary framework for academic inquiry is fundamentally opposed to history building.

Literary criticism and historical criticism do not necessarily work hand in hand. Elements of deconstructionist scholarship can, however, aid in historical construction of the Rabbinic period. But, for any real progress for the construction of Rabbinic history, primary theoretical and academic inquiry must focus on construction and theories for that construction, subjugating literary deconstruction as a tool in that effort. The question still remains – which "school" will succeed in bringing about a fundamental historical framework for Rabbinic history around which academic discourse will revolve?

Write a critique of Green's article "What's in a Name." What are the implications of his argument for the feasibility of producing a history of the rabbinic period, and how would you propose to deal with these limitations?

In his article,[6] Green concludes that no Rabbinic biography could be written nor even an intellectual biography. Green explains that this is supported in the examination of motives of the redactors and the literary structure of Rabbinic works. The only thing that can be assessed through the Rabbinic sources, according to Green, is "a cross-section of rabbinic culture." By this, Green refers to "the internal process of rabbinic tradition" (p. 89). The implication of his argument and conclusion is that no viable history of the rabbinic period can be done. I disagree with Green's position and would like to argue that one can produce a history of the Rabbinic period and Rabbinic biography can function as an important tool in this regard.

I would like to start by elaborating on Green's position that no Rabbinic biography nor intellectual biography could be written. Green's argument hinges on two points; namely, motive and literary form. Green argues that the motive behind the composition of the Rabbinic documents was for the redactors of the documents to prop up their authority and offer themselves as a substitute authority for the displaced priestly authority due to the destruction of the Jerusalem Temple in 70 AD. In the wake of the disappearance of the Jerusalem Temple cult, the upholders of early Rabbinic Judaism shifted emphasis of holy life centered around it and emphasized its application everywhere.

---

[6] W. S. Green, "What's in a Name? – The Problematic of Rabbinic Bibliography," *Approach to Ancient Judaism* (Missoula: Scholars Press, 1978), pp. 77-96.

This shows continuity with the Pharisees and their ideas. Study and exposition became a religious expression for Rabbis to the same extent that any cultic ritual was before the destruction of the Temple. Green writes:

> If the performance of rituals within the Temple exposes the lines of God's revealed reality, then thinking and debating about those rituals outside the Temple, even without the possibility of performing all of them, has the same result. ... Study, learning and exposition, became not only the basic rabbinic activity, but a principal expression of piety as well (p. 78).

Thus, Green describes the chief motive of the Rabbinic literature in terms of its culture: "A principal goal of rabbinic culture was to overcome the vertigo initially brought on by the Temple's destruction and severely intensified by the disaster and failed messianism of the Bar Kokhba rebellion" (p. 79). This motive did not encourage creating the kind of biography that seems to have perpetuated in the contemporaneous socio-historical environment; namely, the hagiography.

Besides the idea that the motive of the Rabbis was not conducive to the creation of biographies, Green argues that even the literary form of the Rabbinic works shows that biography cannot be constructed out of them. Green writes that features of the Rabbinic documents exhibit "agenda" surpassing the teaching of any single sage. First, Rabbinic documents have a lot of non-attributed materials. Second, Rabbinic documents are structured around thematic, formal, topical, or scriptural arrangement with teachings of various sages rather than around the sayings of one individual. Third, preservation and vitality of the teachings depended on the rabbinic circles and communities that transmitted them. In their transmission, they embellished and refined received tradition and even sometimes created new ones to fit their agenda (p. 80). Thus, Rabbinic documents were not particularly interested in the teaching of one particular sage nor in his life.

Furthermore, in Green's argument, particular literary forms of Rabbinic documents exhibit a tendency against constructing Rabbinic biography. Green argues that in Mishnah-Tosefta, sayings and rulings have been cast into rhetorical patterns, even "stereotyped" patterns, in the process of transmission. An example of this form is the "dispute-form" which exhibit two or more Rabbis defining problems in an issue and expressing themselves in identical ways. For Green, such fixture into the "dispute-form" necessitated alteration and modification of language of the sage to whom the saying is attributed and also even of the originally intended meaning (pp. 80-82). Green concludes:

> Forms by nature remove us from a historical figure because they 'package' or epitomize his thought, obscure idiosyncrasy and unique modes of expression, and thereby conceal distinctive

elements of personality, character and intellect. The very presence of forms means at the outset that we cannot claim to have the exact words spoken by any Yavnean master (p. 81).

For Green, therefore, it is axiomatic that the presence of forms and fixture into forms are indicative of the unreliability to the sayings that have become fixed.

Thus, because of motives behind the compilers and the literary form of Rabbinic documents, Green argues that no viable biography of Rabbinic sages nor even an intellectual biography can be written. But Green goes even so far as to say that setting these factors aside, still one would not be able to write a Rabbinic biography because of scarcity of sources. Green writes:

> Even ignoring the critical considerations raised above, any attempt to recover the life of an early Tanna is doomed from the start because of insufficient information. In the strict sense of the term, rabbinic biography is an impossibility (p. 87).

Although Green sees writing Rabbinic biography as an impossibility, he does allow for some possibility of ascertaining information about the Rabbinic past.

According to Green, the only thing that can be assessed through the Rabbinic sources is "a cross-section of rabbinic culture," by which he refers to the internal process of the transmission and redaction of

Rabbinic tradition that provides a picture behind the nature of it. For instance, by studying the description of one stated view of a sage in earlier sources and comparing it with the view of the sage as represented by a later sage, one can see the nature of Rabbinic tradition. How faithful is the later tradition to the individuality of the sage? Green argues that it is the nature of the internal dynamics in Rabbinic tradition that any biographical study of Rabbis might yield (p. 89). Thus, any biographical study would be a study in tradition transmission but is not helpful for gathering accurate information about the actual life or saying of the Rabbis themselves.

The question is, therefore, how did later tradition choose to preserve earlier tradition's portrayal or a sage? The implication is clear. Green does not believe that a viable history of the rabbinic period is possible.

I disagree with Green's position. I would like to argue that one can produce a history of the Rabbinic period, and Rabbinic biography can function as an important tool in this regard. I would first like to argue this point by critiquing Green's position. The main reasons that Green offers for the inability to conduct a biographical study of Rabbinic sages are attributed to motive and literary structure. Green argues that the fact that the Rabbinic documents exhibit an overarching agenda of reshifting Judaism from a Temple-centered religion to a religion based on piety apart from the Temple was an overriding factor that did not value individual Rabbinic contribution. So in this light, sayings and deeds attributed to individual Rabbis must be seen as unreliable. This argument based on motive is faulty.

Just because a document or an author has an agenda does not mean that the contents are wholly unreliable for historical inquiry. In fact, Shaye Cohen goes even far as to say that all inquiry in history are agenda oriented. In "The Modern Study of Ancient Judaism," Cohen writes: "History, like most of the humanities, is art, not science. Its results are conditional, not inevitable; conjectured, not empirical. Historical truths are not 'discovered' so much as 'created' by the interpreter..." (p. 56). In this light, then, no historical inquiry can be done, since all agenda oriented inquiry or study is unreliable, according to Green.

Besides motive, Green argues that the literary structure of the Rabbinic documents discourage writing of Rabbinic biography. Green's primary argument in this regard is that formulas and fixation of saying and deeds into them necessitate changing of the contents to fit them, especially in the "dispute-form" which require scholarly disagreement. This argument is also faulty on the grounds that formula does not necessarily indicate changing of contents.

It is not at all unusual to have a structure to discourse and dispute. In fact, rhetorical training in the ancient world involved, at least in part, learning the structures of rhetoric. It is not at all impossible that the "dispute-form" was the actual discourse format that was employed in Rabbinic learning settings and is preserved in the Rabbinic documents. This seems to be in keeping with several realities in the Rabbinic documents. For one, the disputation form seems consistent throughout the Rabbinic corpus, across time, such as between Mishnah and the Talmuds, and also across genre, such as Halakhic literature and Midrashic literature.

Also, the rabbinic text describes "pairs" who carried on Rabbinic disputation, such as Hillel and Shammai. In the later period, there is the school at Sura and the other one at Pumpadita in Babylonia. Disputation seems to be at the heart of Rabbinic Judaism. To argue that the mere existence of a dispute form necessitates a distortion of the actual sayings and deeds is to argue that all realities described in a dispute form is likely to be spurious. Thus, using this argument of Green, one might argue that even Sura and Pumpadita were literary creations. And this is clearly bordering on the ridiculous. The mere existence of and fixture into forms do not indicate the spurious nature of their contents.

Thus, major reasons offered by Green against Rabbinic compositions – namely, motive and literary structure – do not function as legitimate arguments for dismissing the contents of the Rabbinic documents. In fact, we can produce a history of the Rabbinic period and Rabbinic biography can have an important function in this regard. But we must be careful not to use sources the way Green wants to use them; namely, as having value only as final redactions. This perception of Green causes him to fall into the pitfall of treating Rabbinic documents as wholes, instead of a compilation of parts. For instance, Mishnah is treated as a whole document redacted by Judah the Prince and exhibiting chiefly the interest of his circle. Likewise, the Babylonian

Talmud is perceived as a document reflecting the interest and concerns of the time of the final redaction around 500 AD. In this light, Green sees the Babylonian Talmud as wholly secondary to the Mishnah and dependent on it. Such simplistic way of looking at source criticism and redaction criticism is not helpful in constructing Rabbinic history.

The first step to any constructive Rabbinic history writing is to give due respect to the complexity of Rabbinic sources and of their redaction. Mishnah did function as a source for the Babylonian Talmud. But there might also have been floating separate sources that the Babylonian Talmud utilized, which, in turn, might also have been a source for the Mishnah. Also, one must recognize the possibility that Rabbinic documents went through several stages of redaction. Thus, one cannot presume that the final form of the Jerusalem Talmud was the exclusive source for the Babylonian Talmud in its final redaction stage. Previous versions of the Jerusalem Talmud (no longer available to us) might have functioned as sources at various stages of the redaction of the Babylonian Talmud.

Also, one cannot rule out the possibility that sources preserved in later Talmudic documents could actually be an earlier source than those preserved in earlier Rabbinic documents. For instance, it is theoretically possible that the Babylonian Talmud preserved a tradition from a separately surviving source that might have been ignored by the Mishnah in its final redaction. If this is the case, then the Babylonian Talmud could possibly preserve the tradition of a lost source that is not preserved in

Mishnah, but earlier than it. Thus, just because final redaction of the Babylonian Talmud is later than the final redaction of the Mishnah, this does not necessarily confirm its wholesale secondary nature. All this is to illustrate the need for a three dimensional view of source and redaction criticism and not a two dimensional view that seems to characterize Green.

In light of this complex dynamics, I would prefer to compare separate pericopes dealing with similar stories. In doing so, all possible extant Rabbinic sources will be examined. First, I will identify similarities between these separate versions and isolate them. This common core can be seen as possibly relating to the earliest strata of actual composition. Then, I will examine where there are limited common similarities; i.e., which sources share similarities and which sources are missing this data. Depending on which sources share similarities, a conclusion can be drawn. For instance, if the Mishnah and the Babylonian Talmud share similarities, then it is possible that the tradition will go at least to the Mishnah. If Babylonian Talmud and Jerusalem Talmud share similarities, but no other sources share them, then it would be safe to assume that they belong to the Amoraic period, but it would require some critical argument to state that it might also belong to Tannaitic period or earlier. In this case, we can ask the question – what is it about the Amoraic period that encouraged inclusion (or fabrication) of this tradition common only to the Jerusalem Talmud and the Babylonian Talmud? This question can lead to a conclusion about the historical environment of the Amoraic period. Thus, synoptic treatment would not only aid in conclusion about source primacy, but also in indication of Sitz im Leben of the synoptic similarities and differences, especially in light of the chronological differences among the texts. In this context, motivation or agenda plays a secondary role in commenting on the possible socio-historical environment.

The benefit of this kind of biographical research for historical writing of the Rabbinic period is evident. First of all, common literary core regarding a Rabbinic figure will be identified. This common core can be used in the construction of the biography of the sage. Of course, common literary core does not necessarily equate a historical kernel; on the other hand, one should recognize the usefulness of a biography of a sage, even if he is a literary sage. Would this not be similar to a lot of hagiographic writings that Green alluded to in his article, which were also purported biographies, but resembled literary creations? There were most likely these saintly individuals, but how reliable were stories of their actions? For instance, Simon the Stylite in Syriac Christian tradition was purported to have remained on top of a very high pillar for many years. Simon the Stylite most likely existed, but how reliable is the account of his purported action?

The benefit of the synoptic study is not merely confined to a creation of a biography (based on the collection of literary kernels from several synoptic comparisons of sage pericopes), it is also extended to a greater understanding of the Rabbinic period resulting from the identification and analysis of differences. This benefit can be likened to that found in Medieval History.

The Donation of Constantine was believed to have been a historical fact for many years. It is a document that purported that Constantine in the fourth century AD gave a part of his kingdom to the pope as a gift. This document was meant to prop up the secular power of the pope in the continuing conflict between the papacy and the secular monarch for supremacy in the Middle Ages. Based on the Donation of Constantine, Peppin, the father of Charlemagne, was purported in the eighth century AD to have given his own Donation to the pope, recognizing pope's innate authority over his kingdom. Later on, the Donation of Constantine was found out to be a forgery. However, the existence of Constantine and the fact that he recognized Christianity as a legitimate religion are historical kernels.

There are other elements in the Donation of Constantine that indicate common historical kernel, as well. Where the Donation of Constantine differs with its sources indicates the concerns of the time in which the forgery was made, which was closer to the time of Peppin. The papacy was interested in exerting authority over the secular ruler, so the document shows the secular monarch paying homage to the pope and recognizing the pope's innate dominion over his kingdom. In both the case of the sages of the Rabbinic period and also with the Donation of Constantine, the literary and historical core can be identified and also the picture into the world of the later composition when it deviates from the earlier source.

Thus, it is useful to engage in synoptic study of similar pericopes within Rabbinic literature in an effort to compose a biography of a sage. Carrying out various synoptic studies would provide a collection of common literary kernels. Using these common literary kernels, one could compose a form of biography of the sage. It may not necessarily cover the life of the sage from his birth to his death, but a biography does not necessarily have to be an all inclusive affair. In fact, one could regard the process of combining these various common literary-historical kernels as a historiographical exercise. Having a coherent "biography" of a sage by these means is more useful for the construction of Rabbinic history, since this biography of a sage can be combined with other such biographies.

Equally important in having these common literary-historical kernels and historiographically constructed biographies are the isolated differences, which provide a picture into their Sitz im Leben. These, too, will work toward aiding in the composition of a Rabbinic history. Of course, the question of how to achieve harmonious integration of these varying products into a coherent history requires further rumination. However, all this goes to show the feasibility of writing a Rabbinic history.

Midrash and Method: An Examination of the Most Recent Monographs on Methodology[1]

In this paper, I will consider very recent scholarly works by three leading scholars on Midrash propounding methodology for studying Midrash and their application of that methodology for understanding the community that produced it. There are many books on Midrash and methodology for its study published in the last twenty years. For the purposes of this paper, I will examine the most recent scholarly monographs relating to methodology for studying Midrash published in the last five years. The academic monographs that I will consider are *Midrash and Theory: Ancient Jewish Exegesis and Contemporary Literary Studies* by David Stern,[2] *The Midrashic Process: Tradition and Interpretation in Rabbinic Judaism* by Irving Jacobs,[3] and *The*

---

[1] This paper was written in the context of a doctoral seminar at Harvard Divinity School in 1999. I would like to thank Professor Jon D. Levenson for reading the complete paper and offering helpful comments.
[2] David Stern, *Midrash and Theory: Ancient Jewish Exegesis and Contemporary Literary Studies* (Evanston: Northwestern University Press, 1996).
[3] Irving Jacobs, *The Midrashic Process: Tradition and Interpretation in Rabbinic Judaism* (Cambridge: Cambridge University Press, 1995).

Exegetical Imagination: On Jewish Thought and Theology by Michael Fishbane.[4]

What is common to all these three works is the connection between proposed theory for understanding Midrash and its essential relationship to the perceived reality of the community in which Midrash was produced and/or propagated. As will be shown in this paper, each scholar's methodology represents a vested interest in its relationship to the conclusion not only regarding Midrash but also regarding the Rabbinic community. The theory that each scholar chose, or created, provides the rationale for his statements regarding Rabbinc Judaism. In this light, I would like to see this paper as a survey of the most recent scholarship on methodology for studying Midrash and an examination of the connection between methodology and conclusions regarding the socio-historical realities of the Rabbinic community which produced Midrash.

First, I will consider David Stern's theory for studying Midrash and its implication for understanding the community in which it was produced. Stern's theory is heavily influenced by modern literary theory. In fact, Stern argues that the study of Midrash requires interaction with modern literary theory for a comprehensive understanding of Midrash. In this light, Stern proposes a theory for the study of Midrash that is dependent on the modern literary theory relating to the "literature of interpretation," a

---

[4] Michael Fishbane, *The Exegetical Imagination: On Jewish Thought and Theology* (Cambridge: Harvard University Press, 1998).

genre[5] to which Stern appends Midrash. In particularizing the theory to Midrash, Stern argues that Midrash is characterized by polysemy – a variety of interpretations that is allowed to co-exist. For Stern, this assessment is important in understanding the nature of the origin of Midrash as well as the community in which it was composed.[6] I will elaborate on these points of Stern in the following paragraphs.

Indeed, for Stern, literary theory is a key to unlocking the mystery of Midrash. In this vein, Stern applauds the recent trend in the study of Midrash in incorporating current literary theory into the study of Midrash. Stern notes that although modern academic study of Midrash began with the Wissenschaft des Judentums couple centuries ago,[7] the initial interest in utilizing literary theory for the study of Midrash began some fifteen years ago.[8] Stern implies that

---

[5] James Kugel prefers not to use the term "genre" in describing Midrash, but rather wants to define Midrash as a method of study. Kugel writes: "At bottom midrash is not a genre of interpretation but an interpretative stance, a way of reading the sacred text..." ("Two Introductions to Midrash," *Midrash and Literature*, ed. Geoffrey H. Hartman and Sanford Budick [New Haven: Yale University Press, 1986, pp. 77-103] 91).

[6] Gerald L. Bruns argues that interpretation often necessarily corresponds to contemporary human concerns. Midrash, for Bruns, is helpful in illustrating this. Bruns writes: "Midrash gives us an insight into what interpretation always is (whatever the method) when interpretation *matters* to human life: In hermeneutical terms, midrash shows the historicality of understanding" ("Midrash and Allegory: The Beginnings of Scriptural Interpretation," *The Literary Guide to the Bible*, ed. Robert Alter and Frank Kermode [Cambridge: Harvard University Press, 1987, pp. 625-645] 632).

[7] Stern 7.

[8] Stern 15.

greater influence of literary theory on the academic study of Midrash is a positive trend in that it provides a neutralizing element to the "identity politics of Jewish studies." Stern states that the modern study of Midrash since Zunz of the Wissenschaft des Judentums has been influenced by an interest in creating a secular Jewish identity using "foundational texts of the past." This is a part of the trend in modern critical study of Judaism in shaping "Jewish selfhood" in the modern world.[9] Using literary critical theory, then, would provide a more neutral study of the texts.

In fact, Stern uses stronger language to describe the contribution of modern literary theory for understanding Midrash. Stern writes that understanding Midrash "was made possible only through exposure to modernist writers and critics like Franz Kafka, Jorge Luis Borges, Walter Benjamin, and Roland Barthes, whose writings similarly compound text and exegesis. If we had not first learned how to read these modernists, we would never have known how to read midrash."[10] Thus, modern literary theory is crucial in providing a methodological tool for the study of Midrash.[11]

---

[9]Stern 9-10.
[10]Stern 8.
[11]Acknowledging the benefits of modern literary theory for the study of Midrash, Ithamar Gruenwald emphasizes the contribution that the study of Midrash as a genre has for the study of literature in general. Gruenwald writes: "Indeed, scholars and literary critics have gradually realized that Midrash as a literary genre and form of interpretive expression is prsent in almost all form of literary creation, and that the study of Midrash raises hermeneutical questions that have interesting consequences for the study of literature and philosophy" ("Midrash and the

For Stern, the central benefit of the joining of Midrash and modern literary theory, then, is the identification and understanding of the genre of Midrash as a "literature of interpretation." Stern does not use the term "genre" but the fact that this is his meaning is evident when he writes: "But what was most remarkable about this new perception [is] the ability to see the process of interpretation not only as the method but also as the very essence of the literary nature of midrash."[12] And central to characteristics of Midrash as a literature of interpretation is its polysemy nature.

In Midrash, one finds various separate interpretive traditions offered side by side. Not only is there a variety of interpretations, often these interpretations exist together without a judgment as to which one is right and which one is wrong.[13] This, therefore, points to the belief of the composers, or

---

'Midrashic Condition': Preliminary Considerations," *The Midrashic Imagination: Jewish Exegesis, Thought, and History*, ed. Michael Fishbane [Albany: State University of New York Press, 1993, pp. 6-22] 6).

[12] Stern 8.

[13] Moshe Idel notes that one of the reasons why diversity of meanings was possible in Midrash is that there is no tendency to systematic theologizing in Midrash. This allowed the composers of Midrash "to manipulate the text as a literary work" (Moshe Idel, "Midrashic versus Other Forms of Jewish Hermeneutics: Some Comparative Reflections," *The Midrashic Imagination: Jewish Exegesis, Thought, and History*, ed. Michael Fishbane [Albany: State University of New York Press, 1993, pp. 45-58] 53).

compilers, of Midrash that Scripture did not have one meaning, but was open to a variety of meanings.[14] When there is a judgment as to the preference of an interpretation, it is often not on the basis of its correctness. In fact, preference was shown to a more tolerant position. In this regard, Stern writes concerning the preference for the Hillelite position:

> In other words, the halakhah was eventually decided according to the opinion of the House of Hillel not because its teachings were any more correct or valid than those of the House of Shammai, but for ethical reasons. Even though the House of Hillel disagreed with its opponents, it treated the House of Shammai with respect.[15]

This preference for the more tolerant position is in keeping with the very polysemy nature of Midrash. Differences in interpretation are seen as positive, and those who respect differences in interpretation are in keeping with the spirit of the compilers of Midrash and, therefore, given a favorable ruling.

---

[14] Günter Stemberger states that the belief in the existence of multiple meaning in Scripture, as attested in Midrash, is foundational to Rabbinic thinking. Stemberger writes: "Die Rabbinen gehen vom Grundsatz aus, daß jeder Bibeltext einen vielfachen Sinn enthält, infolgedessen auch verschiedene Auslegungen gleich richtig sein können..." (*Midrasch: Vom Umgang der Rabbinen mit der Bibel* [München: Verlag C. H. Beck, 1989] 23).

[15] Stern 21.

Scriptural polysemy is, in fact, a characterizing nature of Midrash and the Rabbinic community in which it was produced. On the other hand, the Qumran community, another ancient Jewish community that had an interpretative literature – namely, pesher – did not share this polysemy position. The Qumran community's pesher interpretations tended to be absolutist with one correct interpretation. The reason for the Qumran community's interest in having one correct interpretation is that often interpretation in the Qumran community referred to contemporary events.[16]

Thus, in light of the apocalyptic historical perspective of the Qumran community, interpretation was used as an authoritative explanation for the imminent end. In this regard, Stern points to the similarity between the Qumran community's interpretation and ancient dream interpretation in the ancient Near East. Stern writes:

> The connection between Qumranic pesher and ancient dream interprettation is a virtual commonplace of modern scholarship. Like ancient dream interpretation, with its single-minded desire to unravel the one and only meaning of the dream, pesher

---

[16]Kugel writes: "For midrash, as opposed to Qumranic *peser* and other 'political' exegeses, generally views Scripture as a world unto itself, without a direct connection to our own times..." (90).

interpretation views Scripture as an enigma to be solved and decoded.[17]

Stern provides Pesher Habakkuk as a good example of the Qumran community's absolutist interpretation. But Stern is careful to note that even in Rabbinic equivalent of the Qumran pesher, the petirah, polysemy is evident. The Rabbinic petirah is similar to the Qumran pesher in that it also takes an abstract, ahistorical biblical passage and applies it to a concrete event. However, unlike the Qumran pesher, the concrete events in petirah are not contemporary or from the imminent future, but rather from distant past – often, the biblical past.[18] Polysemy, therefore, characterized Midrash and the Rabbinic community in which Midrash was created.

How do we explain this distinctive and characterizing polysemy of Midrash? Stern perceives that the essential polysemy nature of Midrash is most easily explained by the way in which Midrash as literature came into existence. For Stern, Midrash represents a literature that was a beneficiary of two traditions; namely, the biblical and the Hellenistic. Furthermore, not only Midrash as literature, but even the Rabbinic community, in which Midrash was created, was their beneficiary. Stern writes: "Rabbinic Judaism is already a mixture, a mingling of Israelite, or biblical, and Greco-Roman elements. And so is its foremost literary creation, midrash."[19] Thus, for Stern, diversity of inherited traditions of

---

[17]Stern 22-23.
[18]Stern 23.
[19]Stern 6.

Rabbinic Judaism is, at least, partly embodied in the polysemy of Midrash.

Another factor that might have contributed to the tendency toward polysemy in Midrash is internal dynamics in ancient Judaism. Stern argues that what concerned the Rabbinic community was actually anxiety over its stability and unity. Thus, Midrash represents a textual reflection of the Rabbinic community's efforts at harmony. Stern writes: "In fact, midrashic polysemy suggests more than just textual stability; it points to a fantasy of social stability, of human community in complete harmony, where disagreement is either resolved agreeably or maintained peacefully."[20] For Stern, therefore, the tolerance for differences on a textual level is a reflection of the socio-historical environment in which Rabbinic Judaism found itself. There were various strands within ancient Judaism alongside Rabbinic Judaism, such as the Qumran community, which also claimed to be the legitimate heir to biblical Israelite religion. Since Rabbinic Judaism, according to Stern, was "not always the most obviously successful," it was in its interest to seek stability inclusive of diversity.[21] Thus, for Stern, the polysemy of Midrash is a picture into the reality of the Rabbinic community in which Midrash was created.

One sees the connection between Stern's methodology in identifying the genre of Midrash as a literature of interpretation and his conclusion not only regarding Midrash, but also regarding the community which produced it. Stern emphasizes utilizing mo-

---

[20] Stern 33-34.
[21] Stern 33.

dern literary theory for examining Midrash as literature. Using this method, Stern identifies the genre of Midrash as a literature of interpretation and polysemy as its distinctive characteristic. Stern concludes that polysemy in Midrash is a picture into how the composition came to take upon itself that distinctive characteristic: first, influences from two traditions – namely, Israelite and Hellenistic – which composed Rabbinic Judaism; and secondly, the diversity in ancient Judaism. Stern's conclusions and their integral connection to his theory reflect his vested interest in his theory.

Like David Stern, Irving Jacobs proposes a theory for modern academic study of Midrash that is essentially connected with his conclusions regarding the community in which Midrash was produced. And like Stern, Jacobs' theory also values literary theory for understanding Midrash. However, unlike Stern, Irving focuses less on the nature of the genre of Midrash as a literature of interpretation and more on how the composition came to take the final form. In this regard, Jacobs forwards two major ideas. First, Jacobs argues that Midrash was created in actual preaching contexts. Second, the expositors of Midrash composed their work based on listener response. That is to say, the knowledge and response of the listeners[22] shaped what materials the composers of

---

[22] This approach of Jacobs stands somewhat opposed methodologically to emphasis by scholars of ideological criticism. Ideological criticism examines how ideology shaped text and how it was, in turn, shaped by source-text in creating a new text. Ideological criticism can be seen as a continuation of the more traditional intelletual history, where different ideas, their creators, and their cause and effect are identified. With

Midrash placed in the composition or excluded from the composition. I will elaborate on these points of Irving in the next few paragraphs. In arguing for listeners as a crucial component in the process of the composition of Midrash, Jacobs is careful to note that Rabbis did not compose Midrash in isolation. For Jacobs, Midrash arose out of contexts in which Rabbis were preaching with sensitivity to their audience.[23] Thus, Rabbis appealed to biblical verses,[24] with which their listeners were

---

ideological criticism, however, the nature and function of authorship is questioned, even including self-criticism in this regard. One scholar who employs this method is Daniel Boyarin. Boyarin writes: "The rabbis were concerned with the burning issues of their day, but their approach to that concern was through the clarification of difficult passages of Scripture. Ideology affected their reading but their ideology was also affected by their reading" (*Intertextuality and the Reading of Midrash* [Bloomington: Indiana University Press, 1990] 19). As can be seen, Jacobs' assertion that the audience participated in shaping Midrash is not of concern. The audience does not play a significant role in the theoretical model that examins how authors/redactors used ideology to compose/recompose the text and in the process had their ideology impacted, even resulting in modification to their ideology.

[23] Bruns agrees emphatically with Jacobs' understanding of Midrash arising out of a social dialogue context. Bruns writes: "[Rabbis'] relationship to the text was always social and dialogical, and even when confined to the house of study (*beit midrash*) it was never merely formalist or analytical" (630).

[24] Stemberger notes that it is possible that Bible-reading in synagogues could have provided a context for formation-process of Midrash. Stemberger states: "Zuvor haben wir die Bibellesung in der Synagoge als wesentliches Element in der Entwicklung der Midraschim genannt" (31).

familiar, in support of their statements.[25] Often, these biblical passages are taken out of their context and applied in seemingly haphazard way without a justification for such application. In other cases, the "plain meaning" of the passages used to support arguments or as the basis of a proem is ignored also without justification or explanation. It could be possible that these midrashic expositions were transmitted defectively. However, Jacobs asserts that it is more likely that no explanation for such use of biblical passages are given because the passages represented a shared body of knowledge by the preacher and his audience.[26]

Indeed, for Jacobs, the audience played a crucial role in the shaping of Midrash. Jacobs takes it as a truism that preachers are influenced by their listeners. Jacobs writes: "In his efforts to influence his audience, a preacher/teacher is invariably influenced by them. His choice of theme is often determined by the circumstances and conditions of his listeners, who also exercise a formative influence on the manner of his presentation. He relies upon their collaboration, their comprehension and presumed knowledge which allow him to leave things unsaid...." [27] Thus, Jacobs perceived common

---

[25]Regarding this, Stemberger writes: "Ein Überblick über die erhaltenen rabbinischen Midraschim zeigt eine auffallende Tatsache: Die Rabbinen haben nicht die ganz Bibel mit derselben Aufmerksamkeit bedacht. Einzelne Schriften und Texte der Bibel sind stets von neuem Gegenstand von Bearbeitung und Kommentar geworden; andere kommen nur am Rande, fast gar nicht oder doch erst sehr spät vor" (27).
[26]Jacobs 1-2.
[27]Jacobs 14.

knowledge of the religious source material as crucial for effective preacher-listener communication that resulted in the composition of Midrash. That common denominator was the Bible.

The common denominator of the Bible was the primary source from which the preacher drew his preaching material. In this light, Jacobs emphasizes the Rabbinic elevation of the Bible to the level of the standard. The authority of that standard was due to divine inspiration attributed to the Bible.[28] But the Rabbinic community did not only perceive the Bible as the revealed word of God valid for eternity, but also elevated the language in which it is written as unique and transcending the ordinary medium of human communication. Therefore, commonplace terms, expressions, and even particles of speech in this divine language were seen as repository of deeper meaning requiring interpretation. It was this emphasis on deeper significance of the biblical message that gained primary attention in exegesis. This emphasis on *derash*, however, did not relegate the plain meaning, or *peshat*, of the biblical text to a

---

[28]David Weiss Halivni argues that this divine authority attached to the Bible gave Midrash its authority, since they are intricately linked in the final form of Midrash. Mishnah, on the other hand, did not have an integral link to the Bible. Since a link to divine authority was not self-evident as in Midrash, Mishnah required theological exposition for it authority. For Halivni, this was, at least in part, a motive behind expositions on the Oral Law, which exhibits much development in the Tamudic literature ("From Midrash to Mishnah: Theological Repercussions and Further Clarifications of 'Chate'u Yisrael,'" *The Midrashic Imagination: Jewish Exegesis, Thought, and History*, ed. Michael Fishbane [Albany: State University of New York Press, 1993, pp. 23-44] 23-25).

place of no importance. Jacobs is careful to note that they were both important for the Rabbinic community.[29]

The importance of the Bible and the relevant elevation of its language as a standard point to a crucial element in Jacobs' argument for assessing content in Midrash that can be identified as being from a "popular" source. For Jacobs, any text composed in a vernacular language, such as Aramaic, points toward its popular use and intention. This stands in opposition to halakhic texts which were meant for official uses. Jacobs writes:

> The 'popular' origin of much of the material in *Genesis Rabbah* is further indicated by the extensive use of Palestinian – or Galilean – Aramaic, which constitutes the major linguistic difference between the halakhic and post-talmudic *midrashim*. Aramaic is employed for the many popular stories and anecdotes, which are a feature of *Genesis Rabbah*. This suggests once again that the popular sermons and expositions of the ancient synagogues, in whatever form they were recorded, were a major source for the material in *Genesis Rabbah*.[30]

The heavy use of this Aramaic along with consonance in content points toward dependence on *Talmud*

---

[29] Jacobs 4.
[30] Jacobs 17.

Yerushalmi. But Jacobs notes that the dependence is not necessarily on the version that is available to us, but perhaps on earlier versions that may be now lost. Using this criterion along with the loan words in Greek and Latin, Jacobs dates Genesis Rabbah to fifth or sixth century. For Jacobs, Genesis Rabbah had to be before the Arab conquest, because if it were afterwards, then Arabic influence will be evident in its language.[31] Thus, one sees that Jacobs theory of audience influence in composition results in his conclusion about the composition of the text and the nature of the community in which Midrash was composed.

The emphasis on audience was, indeed, not confined to Jacobs' understanding of internal Jewish dynamics in text-creation. In fact, the very idea of audience response eliciting certain forms and tendency in Midrash was extended into Jewish-Christian polemics. Jacobs argues that certain positions that Christians took caused the Rabbinic community to reformulate its ideas or redirect them. One example that Jacobs provides concerns messianism. Jacobs states that the fact that Christians interpreted many biblical passages as messianic expectation proof-texts for Jesus caused the Rabbis to redirect their preaching and writing toward historicizing or biblicizing of biblical passages dealing with messianic expectation. This tendency to attach biblical figures to passages dealing with messianic expectation in Midrash is a reflection of Jewish-Christian polemics, according to Jacobs. Jacobs writes:

---

[31] Jacobs 16.

> The 'historicisation' of the psalm as Davidic or Abrahamic was due to polemical considerations. ...Psalm 110 figured in Jewish-Christian polemics already in tannaitic times. The adoption by the Church of the messianic interpretation of the psalm to support and propagate its teaching, may have led to a predictable reaction among the early rabbinic scholars. They transferred the psalm from an eschatological to a historical setting, relating it either to David, or to Abraham....[32]

One sees that Jacobs' emphasis on audience influencing text plays a role in his conclusion regarding the impact of Jewish-Christian polemics in the formation of Midrash. Jacobs' theory, indeed, is intricately linked to his socio-historical conclusions.

To sum up, then, Jacobs puts forward methodology questioning the process by which Midrash was composed. According to Jacobs, rightly valuing the role that the audience played in the process of composition requires examining sources that were utilized. The Bible as a source was a fundamental common source shared by the preacher and the audience. Using this common stock of knowledge, the preacher appealed to particular passages which were familiar to his audience in support of his statements. No expositions were given on the "plain meaning" of the text and often the

---

[32] Jacobs 124.

passage was quoted out of context. The reason for lack of explication of seemingly inappropriate biblical passage as preserved in Midrash does not point to corruption in transmission; rather, it points to the familiarity not only of the text but also in regards to the way in which these particular biblical passages are often applied. Using this idea of active preacher-audience interaction in the formation of Midrash, Jacobs was able to date a Midrashic text – namely, Genesis Rabbah – and comment on the nature of the community in which it was produced. One, therefore, sees the essential relationship between proposed theory of Jacobs for understanding Midrash and the perceived reality of the community in which Midrash was produced and propagated.

Like Stern and Jacobs, Michael Fishbane also proposes a theory that is essentially connected to the understanding of the community in which Midrash was created. However, unlike Stern, who focuses on the genre of Midrash and how that is a picture into the contemporary socio-historical environment and concerns, and also unlike Jacobs, who focuses on the process of literary redaction and its picture into common intellectual property of the community, or its collective memory, Michael Fishbane prefers to focus on the theology of Midrash and its diachronic development over centuries. For Fishbane, there was relative continuity in the fundamental theology of Midrash as well as in the essential literary nature of the development of Midrash. Fishbane goes as far as to indicate that literary development of Midrash was a continuation of the literary tradition of the Bible. To achieve this end, Fishbane utilizes the History of

Religions concept of Myth (and Myth-making) and, to a lesser extent, the relationship between Myth and Ritual. In proposing a theoretical model for the study of Midrash, Fishbane expresses his favor of an integrated study as over against a study that examines a segment of text. For Fishbane, integrating various texts referring to similar teaching would provide a more accurate picture of the whole teaching. Fishbane argues that this kind of study is useful not only for one specific idea, but also for "larger anthological wholes." Fishbane confidently concludes: "Indeed, the meaning of Midrash lies in the interrelation and contextualization of its diverse features." [33] And Fishbane further expounds on his integrated hermeneutics in terms of application. Fishbane writes: "My interest in Jewish hermeneutics therefore turned to 'thick' descriptions of actual cases, and to their literary, exegetical, and theological modalities." [34] Thus, Fishbane seeks to understand "midrashic thought."

In this light, Fishbane argues that the most productive way to understand Midrash is to approach it from the History of Religions perspective in which myth-making elements in Midrash are identified and studied as coherent units within the community in which Midrash was created. For Fishbane, myth making was an essential component of midrashic thought. Fishbane, therefore, argues that there was myth-making in Midrash and that this represents a continuity with the biblical tradition, in which myth-

---

[33]Fishbane ix.
[34]Fishbane ix.

making also played a central role. Fishbane feels so strongly about this connection and common shared nature that he writes critically of anyone opposing the concept of myth making in the Bible. Fishbane writes:

> Among the historical religions, classical Judaism is often characterized by its apparent break with mythology. Indeed, if one nostrum is widely accepted it is just this: that the foundation documents of Judaism, the Hebrew Bible, reflects a primary rupture with the world of myth and myth making .... But such assessments are often based on self-serving assumptions and the restriction of admissible evidence to only part of the stream of tradition.[35]

Fishbane, thus, concludes:

> Let us call to mind that biblical Scriptures are replete with instances of mythic drama which strongly resemble the ancient battle between Marduk and Tiamat (from Mesopotamia) or Ba'al and Yam (their Canaanite counterparts); and that this monotheistic myth remained vibrant throughout the Babylonia exile and long thereafter.[36]

---

[35]Fishbane 22.
[36]Fishbane 22.

For Fishbane, therefore, myth making was an important part of Midrash as well as the Bible. In fact, it was a primary literary means by which two literatures are linked.

For Fishbane, Midrash and the Bible not only share methodology in literary creation – namely, that of myth making. They also share the content of that myth making; that is, the mythic content. Fishbane argues that Rabbinic theology represents exposition, interpretation or allegories of its biblical source. Thus, despite his emphasis on the continuity between the Bible and Midrash, Fishbane treats these two literature as essentially separate. The Bible functions as a source – a mythic source that is reshaped by the compilers of Midrash. Fishbane emphasizes the importance of modern scholars to remember this in examining Midrash. Fishbane writes: "For the latter-day interpreter of interpreters, it is precisely these modes of re-voicing that must be studied in order to understand how second-order discourse derives from the first."[37] The Bible is, therefore, important as a source for Midrash.

However, there are cases in which the Bible was not used as a source. There were instances in which other traditions were used as a source for Midrash. In these cases, Fishbane notes the tendency to biblicize [38] these traditions and give them the

---

[37] Fishbane 1.
[38] Kugel prefers the term "legendizing" to describe this process. For Kugel, this stage is the last and necessary process of the midrashic process. Imaginative stories are created in an effort to explain the biblical account, especially when there is sparcity of

impression that they were somehow tied to the biblical tradition. Thus, Fishbane allows for instantces in Rabbinic literature, in which "we have a *constructed* myth, and not a reconstructed one."[39] The efforts to myth making with biblicizing nature points to the fundamental model of myth making, that takes the Bible as a source. This would point toward the community's interest in theological harmony.

Fishbane gives messianic expectation as one example of theological harmony that fills Rabbinic literature. Myth making regarding messianic hope is consistent in Rabbinic literature, according to Fishbane. Fishbane writes:

> The theme of messianic hope is omnipresent in classical Jewish life and literature. It fills the Talmud and Midrash; is repeated in any number of prayers and rituals; dominates the choice of prophetic lections (*haftarot*) for the Sabbaths and festivals; and structures homiletic perorations as well as poetic prayers (*piyyutim*) for the liturgical year.[40]

Furthermore, it reflects what the Rabbinic community perceived as consistent with messianic emphasis in biblical tradition.

---

detail. These created stories would then become a part of the text itself. In this process, distinction lines between the biblical account and the interpretive tradition becomes blurred (100).
[39]Fishbane 54.
[40]Fishbane 73.

For example, Fishbane discusses the messianic concept in Pesiqta Rabbati 34, 36-37, in which suffering meritoriously saves sinners. Fishbane perceives this as consistent with Isaiah 53, which also has a suffering messianic concept. Removed in time, the Midrash revoices the biblical passage along same theological lines. And this was internal Jewish theological development and not the result of a Christian influence. Fishbane writes: "Undoubtedly, these sources were part of an inner Jewish development of messianic interpretation based on Isaiah 53, the antiquity of which need not be doubted."[41] Fishbane argues that writing of Justin Martyr in *Dialogue with Trypho* confirms this.

Justin Martyr notes that Jews expected a suffering messiah but it was not Jesus. There is multiple attestation also in the internal Jewish tradition regarding a suffering servant. In *'Avqat Rokhel*, there is a textual reference to the Messiah-designate accepting joyfully his suffering to atone for the sins of Israel.[42] Thus, for Fishbane messianic expectation provides a good example of a consistent theology in Rabbinic Judaism.

One sees that for Fishbane diachronic treatment of developments within Judaism is important. Fishbane perceives Rabbinic theology as consistent over a long period of time, especially on larger issues such as messianic expectation. Fishbane notes that myth making in Midrash, and in Rabbinic literature generally, with the Bible as "the foundational and sustaining document of rabbinic Ju-

---

[41]Fishbane 83.
[42]Fishbane 84.

daism"[43] explains such unity in theology over a long period of time. Fishbane's methodology in seeing myth making as a unifying literary technique with the Bible at the center provides a picture into the picture of Rabbinic Judaism which was consistent and stable in its theology. This shows that like Stern and Jacobs, Fishbane's proposed theoretical approach to Midrash is directly related to his conclusions about the community in which it was produced.

All the scholars whom I have considered – David Stern, Irving Jacobs, and Michael Fishbane – propose a theoretical approach to studying Midrash that is integrally linked to their conclusions regarding the socio-historical environment of the Rabbinc community, in which Midrash was composed. This paper has examined each recent scholarly theory and its connection to its conclusions about Rabbinic Judaism. The three scholarly approaches examined in this paper represent three distinctive methodologies to studying Midrash and the community that produced it. There were similarities in their conclusions. However, there were visible differences as well, as is evident in the comparision between Jacobs' and Fishbane's discussions of messianism.

I would like to argue that the most accurate understanding of the Rabbinic community and Midrash can only be achieved by combining the three methodologies. Underlying this contention is my argument that the three different theoretical approaches are mostly complementary, rather than oppositional. In the near future, it would be beneficial to work on a comprehensive theory that

---

[43] Fishbane 124.

examines ways in which these three separate methodologies can be constructively combined for a productive academic examination of Midrash and the community that produced it. In this regard, I would like to quote a popular German aphorism: "Alle gute Dinge sind drei."

The Servitude-Exodus Narrative and the Passover as a Factual Legend: A Study of Genre and a Formulation of a Historical Criteria[1]

The Passover tradition in Exodus 12 with its larger literary framework in the book of Exodus is a scholar's delight. It is fraught with many questions regarding source transmission, literary character, genre, and ritual history. The most common approach to the questions regarding the Passover account in Exodus is literary. Thus, the question is posed: what is the literary framework in which this account is contained. Often, the question is identified with the quest for its literary genre.[2] I will examine various

---

[1] I would like to thank Professor Marc Brettler of Brendeis University for reading the complete draft of this paper and commenting on it. This paper was written in 1997.
[2] William W. Hallo sees the importance of genre in studying ancient literature because of individual authors' adherence to its strict form. For Hallo, genre categories provide a means to compare different literature and to study the biblical texts from the contextual approach – the approach that Hallo himself supports in his book, *The Book of the People* (Atlanta: Scholars Press (Brown Judaic Studies 225), 1991), p. 28. Actually, the whole chapter three is helpful in understanding his contextual approach). One lingering question vis-á-vis the biblical materials in general, and the exodus materials in particular, is the nature of genre. This is, in part, the question that I am exploring in this paper. Since there are so many questions in current scholarship regarding genre categories and the efficacy of genre categories in describing the perception (or experience) of the literature, it is somewhat difficult to embrace the contextual approach – although, in theory, it seems to be, perhaps, the most

theories regarding the nature of the book of Exodus, especially as it relates to the larger context of the Passover narrative in chapter twelve.

After my examination of sundry scholarship, I will forward my thesis that the genre of the literary framework in which the Passover account is contained is history, or factual legend. Israelite servitude and subsequent exodus from Egypt is based on factual event. I will discuss the terms "history" and "factual legend" in an effort to explicate the genre categorization. Then, I will forward my working criteria of negative criterion, coherence, and multiple attestation to support the "genre-fication."

One of the ways the text of Exodus has been approached is as a text containing different documents, or sources. Scholars have identified elements (or differing combinations) of J, E, D, and P as sources for the book of Exodus and the Passover material contained in Exodus 12. Ferdinand Ahuis's book, *Exodus 11,1-13,16 und die Bedeutung der Trägergruppen für das Verstandnis des Passa*,[3] provides a recent treatment of the Passover narrative(s) in Exodus 12 and its immediate literary context in terms of source analysis. Ahuis identifies J, P, and DtrT within Exodus 11:1-13:16. Ahuis writes:

> In Ex 11,1-13,16 lassen sich drei literarische Größen unterscheiden: der Jahwist, die Priesterschrift und eine

---

viable way to approach ancient texts as historical texts in their context.
[3]Göttingen: Vanderhoek & Ruprecht, 1996.

den Jahwisten und die Priesterschrift zusammenfassende deuteronomistische Redaktion des Tetrateuch. Eine Elohist konnte nicht festgestellt werden; ebenso wenig erwies sich eine Annahme von P^s als erforderlich.[4]

This recent assessment of Ahuis stands in contrast to the source analysis of Brevard S. Childs. Childs assigns less prominence to the Deuteronomistic redaction.[5]

Furthermore, Childs and Ahuis disagree on the specifics of the sources within the Exodus tradition. Exodus 12:35-36 provides a good example for comparison. Childs allows the possibility of the E source in Exodus 12:35-6.[6] Ahuis, on the other hand, assigns Exodus 12:35-36 to DtrT.[7] Both assessments of Childs and Ahuis differ from that given by Martin Noth. Noth places Exodus 12:35-36 in the larger J unit of Exodus 12:29-39.[8] The disagreement evidenced here provides a picture into the divergence in scholarly opinion in regards to source analysis.

Some scholars, thus, see the inadequacy of source analysis for the examination of the Passover tradition and Exodus. One such scholar, Thomas L.

---

[4]81.
[5]Brevard S. Childs, *The Book of Exodus: A Critical Theological Commentary* (Philadelphia: The Westminster Press, 1974) 184.
[6]184.
[7]122.
[8]Martin Noth, *Exodus: A Commentary* (Philadelphia: The Westminster Press, 1962) 98.

Thompson, actually wants to dismiss documentary hypothesis, altogether. Thompson writes: "Differences in divine names, place names, references to individuals and groups, even differences in style and language, while often giving evidence for the lack of homogeneity in the tradition, do not justify the positing of distinct documents, separated by centuries."[9] His dissatisfaction compels Thompson to see parts of Exodus (and Genesis) in terms of coherent literary characteristics.

Thompson, therefore, forwards his own literary theory to explain the nature of the Exodus (and Genesis) materials. Thompson introduces the term, "traditional complex-chain narrative," as a narrative genre that is intentional and "...a specific type of oral or literary unit. [that] has its own beginning and end, its own theme, and its own plot-line (i.e. its own developmental direction), which enables it to exist as a literary entity, and to have a life of its own, independent of both its context and the narrative materials from which it is formed."[10] Thompson identifies five "clear and unequivocal examples of this genre,"[11] and posits that the Passover "chain narrative" was composed with this genre in mind.

Thompson's work is helpful in presenting the possibility of examining the Exodus materials, apart from the documentary hypothesis scheme. Thomp-

---

[9]Thomas L. Thompson, *The Origin Tradition of Ancient Israel: The Literary Formation of Genesis and Exodus 1-23* (JSOT Supplement Series 55) (Sheffield: Sheffield Academic Press, 1987) 155.
[10]156-157.
[11]157.

son's work is valuable in that he links literary analysis with genre criticism, and, by its very existence, encourages further examination of the Exodus material(s) in models other than documentary hypothesis.[12] Yet, Thompson does not escape the literary framework that is characteristic of discussing the Passover tradition and the book of Exodus.

Posing questions regarding Passover tradition necessitates placing questions concerning the literary framework in which it finds itself.[13] The central

---

[12] Biblical scholars in other specializations have recently voiced discontent regarding their own methodological approaches to studying texts and referred to their limitations. One such scholar is Burton L. Mack, who writes regarding his examination of Ben Sira's hymn: "I approached the text as a scholar trained in the traditions of biblical criticism, dissatisfied, however, with the limited horizons of understanding customary to this field. It was, I thought, the inadequacy of traditional biblical criticism in general to read a text specifically in relation to its contingent, complex social context that accounted for its failure in the case of Ben Sira's hymn. What appeared to be needed was a larger frame of reference to help with the phrasing of questions. This I discovered to be in the making in recent discourse in the academy. There it has begun to be thought that in order to understand a text, it must be seen as part of a larger system of signs. The insight comes from the early scholars of structural linguistics, of course. But it now pervades studies across the range of the humanities and human sciences seeking relations among the several fields. This discourse is learning to treat religion and culture, literature and society, as complex, interrelated systems of signs. Regarding them as "texts," the scholarly endeavor is to "read" them together, "translating" from system to system, and so come to understand their "meaning" (*Wisdom and the Hebrew Epic* [Chicago and London: The University of Chicago Press, 1985] 5).

[13] It would also be possible to approach the question of the Passover from a myth-ritualist theory of religion perspective.

question, therefore, is one that pertains to the genre of the literature. It is my assertion that the text of Exodus containing servitude and exodus from Egypt is history, or factual legend.[14] Without being bogged

---

For a good synopsis of the internal discussion, see Robert A. Segal, "The Myth-Ritualist Theory of Religion," *Journal for the Scientific Study of Religion* 19/2 (1980) 173-185. Also, Heinz Reinwald's *Mythos und Method: Zum Verhältnis von Wissenschaft, Kultur und Erkenntnis* (München: Wilhelm Fink Verlag, 1991) provides a good discussion of current methodology, especially as pertaining to the classical world of Greece. Yet, one needs to be careful in utilizing methodology regarding myth and/or ritual that has Greece as its primary point of reference, since our perception is, in part, shaped by the Greek tradition (particularly philosophical) that perceived myths as innately untrue.

[14] In discussing legends, one may draw analogies from the modern era – for instance, the American Thanksgiving. One good discussion of legend (or "mythic narrative") in regards to the American Thanksgiving celebration is Bruce Lincoln's article, "Mythic Narrative and Cultural Diversity in American Society" in *Myth and Method*, edited by Laurie L. Patton and Wendy Doniger (Charlottesville and London: University Press of Virginia, 1996). Lincoln's discussion focuses on the movie, *Avalon*, written and directed by Barry Levinson. Lincoln uses the movie to show how the Thanksgiving dinner becomes an opportunity for those in America for relating (and re-relating) the meaning of the Thanksgiving in their own personal (or clan) experience. Thus, Lincoln shows by argument and by analogy (to the movie) how mythic narrative is shaped. In my assessment, this type of study can enlighten our understanding of the Passover narrative, ritual, and inter-relationship between them, but only to an extent. For one, the Thanksgiving experience in the context of American society is seen as collective experience within a multicultural (multiracial and multireligious) context. Thus, Lincoln presents individualizing elements in the mythic narrative as an axiom in the American context. On the other

down with every aspect of the Exodus account or with the supernatural accounts placed therein, I would like to ask larger questions regarding the genre and why I am asserting that the genre is history,[15] or factual legend.[16]

I am using the term "history" interchangeably with the term "factual legend." Since having been trained in modern critical scholarship, we are prone to think of history in terms defined by western

---

hand, I would posit that the Passover ritual (and narrative) had a collectivizing force. This, in my assessment, is due to the actuality of the Passover experience (ritual) in Egypt and its garnered collective social and literary consciousness, maintaining the value and actuality of the Passover in Egypt. Thus, *Pesach Dorot* is reactualization, but also a reaffirmation, of the *Pesach Mizraim*.

[15]Hallo encourages looking at the whole picture of the Exodus, rather than in parts. Hallo writes: "...it helps to analyze the biblical book, not into the original documents which (by the documentary hypothesis or other critical estimates) went into its making, but into its major generic components. Reading the text in its "canonical" shape, that is as a single, finished work of literature, one tends to detect three such components – biography, history and legislation" (46). Hallo identifies chapters 7-17 as history (47).

[16]Hallo seems to place history and legend in opposition. Hallo writes: "To turn from Genesis to Exodus is, then, to pass from legend to history" (47). Hallo basically defines legend (along with myth and novella) as "the formulation of what *may* have been, the almost random choice of one or more explanations for the present state of affairs in terms of their possible origins and of selected intervening stages, told by preference in the form of biographical details associated with paradigmatic individuals" (45-46, *italics his*) and history as "what *must* have been: the necessary organization of group traditions into a meaningful sequence of events that can account for the group's present awareness of its collective destiny" (46, *italics his*).

scholarship of last couple centuries. But should history be seen necessarily as distinct from legend? On the surface, placing history and legend in the same category as synonymous expressions seems to be a confusion of literary and historical approaches to the study of texts. This seeming contradiction is more indicative of the current approaches in biblical studies, rather than to their inherent opposition.

Marc Brettler has noted the current dichotomy between literary and historical approaches to biblical studies. Brettler writes: "Most scholars who are interested in applying models from literary studies have little interest in the history of Israel, while most historians look askance at literary studies of the Bible as antihistorical. Few scholars have realized that these two disciplines may, in certain cases, be mutually enlightening." [17] Thus, in his article, Brettler uses "literary-historical" approach to examine the historical factors that influenced the editor(s) of Judges to give the work its final shape. In the similar spirit of understanding compatibility, or "mutual-enlighten-ability," of history and literature, I have defined "factual legend" as a qualitative equal to "history" in describing genre category of the Exodus account bearing the servitude-exodus account, with the Passover narrative as a central theme.

Before examining further the qualitative compatibility of the terms, "history" and "factual legend," it would be helpful to note the legitimacy of the compatibility based on the reality that definition of history and approaches to history (which is, to an

---

[17] Marc Brettler, "The Book of Judges: Literature as Politics," JBL 108/3 (1989) 395.

extent, the same thing) are, indeed, not universally defined or agreed to.
Indeed, the understanding or definition of history is not monolithic. Even German scholarship points out the distinction between *Historie* and *Geschichte*, the former being the actual event and the latter being the accounting of that event. Both could be translated as "history" in English, although many have preferred to translate it as "historical event" and "historiography," in light of the scholarly connotations. German scholarship's distinguishing between two "histories" is tantamount to their acceptance of nuances in the innate reality of history. For, even talking about the "historical event," one may pose the question, what does it mean by an event that actually or historically happen? Despite the seemingly neat categorization of *Historie* and *Geschichte*, the lines become quickly blurred, when one attempts to describe what it means for an event to actually take place. In fact, *Historie* is a theoretical reality that is only describable in terms of *Geschichte*. Both terms, therefore, fail to fulfill their *raîson-être* of effectively demarcating differences in the idea of history.

The nuance of the term "history" is also highlighted in Yosef Hayim Yerushalmi's comment that if Herodotus was the father of history, then Jews are the first to seek meaning behind history.[18] First of all, what does it mean to be the father of history? Second of all, is not seeking meaning behind history a form of history? Third of all, is the term history here referring to historiography? If so, then is

---

[18] Yosef Hayim Yerushalmi, *Zachor: Jewish History and Memory* (Seattle: University of Washington Press, 1982) 8.

Yerushalmi saying that the Jews are the first to conduct historiography (finding meaning) of historiography ("history")? By his very statement, Yerushalmi is, in fact, recognizing different connotations, or even denotations, of history.

Even in current academic pursuit of history, scholars seek to reconstruct the past with various methodologies. There are intellectual, ideological, sociological, social historical, political, economic, deconstructionist, and urban historical methodologies – all purporting to be the best way to arrive at the reality of the past. On one level, this dissension reflects a differing understanding of history and what sources and methodologies are most effective in understanding the past.

In light of the lack of consensus on the idea of "history," my equation of history and factual legend in describing the genre of the Exodus account, particularly as it relates to the theme of servitude-exodus with Passover as the central idea, is hardly far-fetched. In the reality of the ancients, legends provided them with a connection to the past and understanding of it. In terms of facticity, legends do not have to be fictitious, but can be factual.

It will be useful to work with a definition of legends. William Bascom defines:

> *Legends are prose narratives which, like myths, are regarded as true by the narrator and his audience, but they are set in a period considered less remote, when the world was much as it is today.* Legends are more often secular than

sacred, and their principal characters are human. They tell of migrations, wars and victories, deeds of past heroes, chiefs, and kings, and succession in ruling dynasties.[19]

Looking at Bascom's definition, one sees that the legends were perceived by the narrator and the audience as true.

Of course, their perception as true does not necessarily mean that the contents are true, but, on the other hand, it does not mean that the narration is false, either. Legends are particularly close to factual accounting because of the contents' proximity to the time of the narrator and his audiences.

In this, myths may be contrasted with legends. Myths are set in remote, often timeless, past. In fact, Bascom describes:

> *Myths are prose narratives which, in the society in which they are told, are considered to be truthful accounts of what happened in the remote past. They are accepted on faith, they are taught to be believed, and they can be cited as authority in answer to ignorance, doubt, or disbelief.*[20]

---

[19] "The Forms of Folklore: Prose Narratives," *Sacred Narrative: Readings in the Theory of Myth* (Berkeley and Los Angeles: University of California Press, 1984, pp. 5-29) 9. *italics his*
[20] 9. *italics his*

Not only are myths different from legends in that myths are set in remote, even timeless, past, and legends are set in a setting considerably less remote, in a world similar to that of the narrator, myths have a different function from legends. Myths function dogmatically as sacred texts, buttressing a belief-system, whereas legends describe events that can often be secular in nature, although sacred elements possibly enter into them.

It is in light of this understanding of legends, I choose to define the genre of the Exodus, especially of the servitude-exodus account with the Passover account, as a legend. I am adding the descriptive adjective, "factual," to "legend" in order to highlight the reality of the servitude-exodus account. Together, the term "factual legend" operates functionally as an alternative definition for, or a type of, history. To phrase this in another way, factual legend as a genre is historiography that recounts the past as it actually happened with some literary embellishments. Although it is not the purpose of this paper to identify what those embellishments are, such study may also yield constructive results in the greater understanding of "factual legends" as a genre.

My thesis that the servitude and exodus account of the framework in which the Passover account finds itself is history, or factual legend, is based on a set of working criteria – namely, those of negative criterion, cohesion, and multiple attestation.

The first criterion, namely that of the negative criterion, also confirms the reality of servitude and exodus from Egypt. First, I will define what I mean by negative criterion, and how an event satisfies this criterion. By negative criterion, I refer to a criterion by which an event shows the unlikeliness to be recorded and transmitted in history. Thus, an event satisfies this criterion if an event, such as one that is shameful, is recorded and transmitted by the community for which it is disadvantageous to do so. The servitude and exodus from Egypt satisfies this negative criterion, because there is no advantage for the ancient Israelites to preserve an account of its abject servitude.

This is poignant in light of the fact that this is a legend about the birth of Israelites as a community. The sons of Jacob, or Israel, descend to Egypt on account of various factors surrounding the ascent of Joseph to a high position in Egypt. Jacob's familial clan is representative of the future community of Israelites. We are led to believe by the legend that the Israelite community had its birth in servitude in Egypt. This stands in stark contrast to myths (and positive legends) regarding the birth of a nation, like Romulus and Remus.

The servitude in Egypt is emphasized in Exodus as well as in other books of the Hebrew Bible. William W. Hallo notes:

> It is in the legislative context, both inside and outside Exodus, that the oppression is most emphasized. The Decalogue insists "remember that you were a slave in the land of Egypt" (Deut. 5:15), and "for you were strangers in the land of Egypt" is a refrain in

all the other law codes (22:20, 23:9; cf. Lev. 19:34, Deut. 10:19).[21]

Thus, not only is there a lack of effort to cover up this shameful part of Israelite history, there is a tendency to highlight it, especially in legal codes.

The fact that the account of servitude and exodus from Egypt, a source of shame, is preserved by the Israelite community points to the factual account of these two themes. John Bright writes:

> Although there is no direct witness in Egyptian records to Israel's presence in Egypt, the Biblical tradition demands belief: it is not the sort of tradition any people would invent! Here is no heroic epic of migration, but the recollection of shameful servitude from which only the power of God brought deliverance.[22]

Also, a significant factor is that Egypt was a neighbor of Israelites. Israelites chose to continue to preserve this account, which was surely a source of shame before the Egyptians.

The second criterion is that of coherence. The themes of servitude in Egypt and Exodus from Egypt is a pervasive thematic concept that coheres in biblical literature. William W. Hallo expounds on the

---

[21] 51-52.
[22] *A History of Israel* (Third Edition) (Philadelphia: Westminster Press, 1981) 121.

extensiveness of the coherence of this historical theme:

> The narrative portions of Exodus include the common experience of the Egyptian oppression, the dramatic escape from Goshen and from the pursuing Egyptians, the first wanderings in Sinai, and the collective assent there to a code of laws – in short, all the constitutive elements of Israel's emergence except for the conquest of the Promised Land. These events run like colored threads through all the rest of biblical literature, becoming paradigms and archetypes for the biblical conception of all of Israelite history.[23]

The coherence of the historical theme of servitude-exodus is, in fact, strengthened by the fact that it is distinctive in nature, when compared to its Near Eastern context. Hallo writes:

> ...they recur in no other Near Eastern historiography. .... No other people preserved a record of its own enslavement, or of 'despoiling' its oppressors by stealth, or of its grudging farewell to the 'fleshbpots of Egypt' (16:3; cf. Num. 16:13 where Egypt is even referred to as a 'land flowing with milk

---

[23] 50.

and honey') or finally of its collective entry into a social compact.²⁴

For Hallo, it is the very uniqueness that "argues in favor of their authenticity; at least they are not imitations of foreign models."²⁵ Thus, uniqueness of the servitude-exodus tradition and its coherence within the biblical text provides a viable criterion for forwarding the argument of the historicity of the tradition.

The first two criteria, individually, can be affirming of the servitude-exodus tradition as historical. Indeed, Bright claims so for the criterion, which I am calling, "negative criterion." Also, Hallo affirms that the uniqueness of the servitude-exodus tradition points to its historicity. Hallo's argument for uniqueness is a part of what I am referring to as the criterion of cohesion, since it is uniqueness "holding together" within biblical tradition in an integrated way that provides an argument for the servitude-exodus tradition's historicity. If these two criteria individually can function to affirm the historicity of the servitude-exodus tradition, how much more so when operating together?

These two viable criteria are further strengthened in light of the criterion of multiple attestation. The Passover tradition is well attested in the Hebrew Bible.²⁶ The attestation of the tradition is evidenced

---

²⁴50-51.
²⁵51.
²⁶Some have posited the lack of multiple attestation outside of the Hebrew Bible in contemporaneous ancient sources as an argument against the historicity of the servitude-exodus account

in the attestation of the term, "Passover." There are forty-six attestations of the word "Passover" in the Hebrew Bible. The Torah has ample attestations (Exodus 12:21, 27, 43, 48; Exodus 34:25; Leviticus 23:5; Numbers 9:2, 4, 5, 6, 10, 12, 13, 14; Numbers 28:16; Numbers 33:3; Deuteronomy 16:1, 2, 5, 6). In view of the history of the Hebrew language, the term, "Passover" is attested in Early Biblical Hebrew texts (2 Kings 23:21, 22, 23) and Late Biblical Hebrew texts (seventeen times in the books of Chronicles, and in Ezra 6:19, 20) as in the transitory text of Ezekiel (45:21).[27]

The multiply-attested term, "Passover," has coherence. The term, "Passover," is used both for the sacrificial animal of the Passover (Exodus 12:21, 27; Exodus 34:25; Leviticus 23:5; Numbers 28:16; Deuteronomy 16:6; 2 Chronicles 30:15; 2 Chronicles 35:6, 7, 8, 11,13; Ezra 6:20) and for the celebration,

---

in Exodus. William W. Hallo objects to this criterion for historicity. Hallo writes: "...these claims [to the historical validity of Exodus] are made strictly in the context of Israel's own formulations. Their neighbors had different preoccupations, and what was crucial to the Israelite historian was more likely than not outside or beneath the notice of any other people's chronicler" (46). James K. Hoffmeier, actually, tries to address the issue of the lack of proof from Egypt. He defines his scope of study: "Here I will examine the main points of the story line described in Genesis and Exodus to see if they are plausible within the limits of our present knowledge of ancient Egypt" (*Israel in Egypt: The Evidence for the Authenticity of the Exodus Tradition* (New York: Oxford University Press, 1997) 53).
[27] Avi Hurvitz's research on the criteria for identifying Late Biblical Hebrew is particularly helpful not only for understanding linguistic development, but in positing historical reality.

called "Passover" (all the other occurrences in the Hebrew Bible). The two meanings for the term are consistently used throughout different document stages of the Hebrew Bible. Thematically, the passages show common ground in that the Passover is an important celebration that needs to be kept (Leviticus 23:5; Numbers 9:2; Deuteronomy 16:1-2; 2 Chronicles 30:5; Ezekiel 45:21). And it is because of the Lord's guiding exodus of Israelites out of the Land of servitude that the Israelites were to celebrate the Passover (Exodus 12:27; Numbers 33:3; Deuteronomy 16:1, 6).

Although, on a certain level, coherence and multiple attestation function together, the very reality of multiple attestation (apart from analysis of coherence) of the term is significant in showing usage and relevance of the term. Thus, multiple attestation of the term "Passover" in the Hebrew Bible[28] works to support the historicity of the event, especially in light of the negative criterion and the criterion of cohesion.

---

[28] Non-biblical texts of the Second Temple period shows concern over Passover observance. Tannaitic literature shows continued stress on the observance of the Passover. Although there is variance in the details of the observance in the Mishnah from the Biblical accounts, the theme of servitude in Egypt and exodus from Egypt continues to be central. The Amoraitic literature further elaborates on the Mishnaic account, and its care for detail, especially in terms of teaching of the young, shows the continued preservation of the theme of servitude in Egypt and exodus from it. For a discussion of the literature, see Baruch M. Bokser's *The Origins of the Seder: The Passover Rite and Early Rabbinic Judaism* (Berkeley and Los Angeles: University of California Press, 1984).

In light of the three criteria, the servitude and exodus theme and the literary framework of the Passover, indeed, can be identified as history, or factual legend. The Passover celebration is integrally tied to the theme of servitude and exodus. It is God who brought them out of Egypt, and the Passover meal celebrates this reality.

If Israelites were interested in fictional legend writing regarding their origin, there are many ways to achieve that in a positive light without placing their origin in the servitude in Egypt. In its current form, the historical legend, at one level, de-legitimizes ancient Israelites' possession of the land of Israel, by portraying them as foreigners to it. Their annual celebration of the Passover is a reminiscence of their foreignness in the land. Thus, although one can pose questions regarding the supernatural accounts and particular details of the servitude and exodus history which contains the Passover celebration, one cannot easily dismiss the possibility of the historical event of servitude-exodus with the Passover tradition. William W. Hallo writes: "The Exodus in particular had such a perennial impact on later Israelite belief and thought that to reject its historicity is to rob subsequent (and even prior) Biblical historiography of its basic paradigm."[29]

---

[29] 107.

A Window into the Deuteronomistic World: Royal Ideology, Zion Theology, and Social Justice as Texts in Judges 19-21[1]

The Judges 19-21 pericope represents a classic Deuteronomistic polemic for Royal Ideology and Zion Theology. Inherent in these two Deuteronomistic ideas is an emphasis on political and religious centralization. This emphasis is clearly evident in the pericope, with politically centralized power taking precedence over religious authority. Yet, the pericope exhibits Deuteronomistic understanding that religious centralized power supports politically centralized power; thus, the pericope describes efforts to prop up religious authority and not undermine it. In order to achieve these classical Deuteronomistic emphases, the writers of the Judges 19-21 pericope utilize various literary tools – such as the inversion of hospitality theme, clever manipulation of sources, especially Genesis 19, and framing the narrative with a "judgment formula." Although Royal Ideology and Zion Theology are important motifs, or "texts," in the Judges pericope, one can also isolate social justice as an important concern, or "text," of the Deuteronomists in the pericope.

Thematically, Royal Ideology is of central concern in the Judges 19-21 pericope. Royal Ideology's central contention is that the Royal House of

---

[1] This paper was written in the context of the Ph.D. program in Judaic Studies at Brown University in 1999.

David will stand forever. Therefore, it is innately a pro-Davidic concept. The Judges 19-21 pericope is pro-David in that it is anti-Saul. The whole pericope is structured to paint Saul's tribe of Benjamin in a negative light. Benjaminite tribe members are inhospitable, stand for injustice, willing to harm other Israelites on account of injustice, and require mercy of the Israelites who have to go out of their way to save their existence.

Hospitality theme in Judges 19-21 has interested quite a number of scholars. Susan Niditch argues that the episode involving inhospitality in Gibeah by the Benjaminites is contrasted by previous episode in Bethlehem (Judges 19:3-10).[2] In that episode, when the man from the tribe of Levi in Ephraim goes to Bethlehem, to the house of his concubine's father, in an effort to win his concubine back, his father-in-law shows inordinate hospitality. For three days, the Levite feasted in his father-in-law's house at his behest. On the fourth day, when the Levite gets up to leave, his father-in-law persuades him to stay for a meal, then to spend another night. The next day, the father-in-law again is overly hospitable and persuades him to stay until the afternoon, so again they share a meal. Towards the evening, the concubine's father tries to persuade the Levite to stay another night. This time, the Levite refuses and starts on his way.

This abundance of hospitality stands in stark contrast to the following episode in Gibeah in

---

[2] Susan Niditch, "The 'Sodomite' Theme in Judges 19-20: Family, Community, and Social Disintegration," CBQ 44 (1982) 366-367.

Benjamin (Judges 19:14-26). No Benjaminite offers hospitality to the Levite and his concubine. In fact, we find the Levite and his concubine in a pitiable scene of sitting in the highly visible city square. Niditch describes this scene as "a perfect expression of his stranger status and his lack of acceptance."[3] When the offer of hospitality finally comes, it is from an old man from the hill country of Ephraim, the hometown of the Levite. Yairah Amit argues that the fact that the old man from Ephraim is a "stranger, who was not a part of the local inhabitants"[4] highlights Benjaminite inhospitality in Gibeah.

Not only does the Levite and his entourage experience lack of hospitality from the Benjaminites in Gibeah, the hospitality that they experience by a non-Benjaminite in the city is interrupted abruptly by what Niditch calls, "the radical, active, and violent 'inhospitality.'"[5] Some men of Gibeah surrounded the house and demanded to have the Levite, in order to have sex with him. Niditch argues that this is particularly significant in light of ancient Israelite injunction against homosexuality, such as found in Leviticus 18:22.[6] Niditch notes: "The threat of homosexual rape is thus a doubly potent symbol of acultural, non-civilized behavior from the Israelite point of view. It is an active, aggressive form of inhospitality."[7] The owner of the house refuses and

---

[3] Niditch 367.
[4] Yairah Amit, *The Book of Judges: The Art of Editing*, tr. Jonathan Chipman (Leiden: Brill, 1999) 344.
[5] Niditch 367.
[6] Niditch 368.
[7] Niditch 369.

offers his virgin daughter and the Levite's concubine for the mob to do with them as they want. When the townsmen did not take the offer, the Levite pushes his concubine outside. The Benjaminite men of Gibeah rape and abused her throughout the night, and they leave her dead in the morning.[8]

Not only do the authors of the Judges 19-21 pericope portray Benjaminites in Gibeah as inhospitable people, even practicing active, aggressive "inhospitality," they also portray the whole tribe as standing for injustice. In the following scene (Judges 19:27-20:16), upon reaching home the Levite from the hill country of Ephraim cuts up his dead concubine's body into twelve parts. Then, he sends the twelve body part pieces to all the areas of Israel. The response is that of horror. The horror is accenttuated by the Israelites' claim that they have not seen anything so horrible since the day that they came out of Egypt. They want the Levite to tell them what to do. The Israelites gather at Mizpah, hear the story of what happened from the Levite, who describes the event with words filled with powerful imagery, such as that of death and killing (v. 5). The Levite also highlights the gravity of the wrong done by Benjaminites in Gibeah by explaining his action of cutting up the concubine's body and sending the pieces to all areas of Israel as a response corresponding to

---

[8]Gale A. Yee allows for the possibility that the woman might not have been dead after the mob rape, since the pericope does not explicitly mention her death. ("Ideological Criticism: Judges 17-21 and the Dismembered Body," *Judges and Method: New Approaches in Biblical Studies*, ed. Gale A. Yee [Minneapolis: Fortress Press, 1995, pp. 146-170] 165).

the horrible deed (v. 6). Thereupon, the Levite asks for a just verdict. The Israelites decide to dispense justice to the perpetrators in Gibeah. And the Israelites offer one tenth of their men to bring this justice about. With this resolve for justice, the Israelites send message to the tribe of Benjamin to deliver up the wrongdoers in Gibeah to receive the death penalty. Benjaminites refuse to give them up to the justice decided on by the collective Israel and organize soldiers to fight against their fellow Israelites to protect the accused. Amit argues that in this act the whole tribe of Benjamin became implicated in the evil deed. Amit writes:

> The points of criticism raised thus far are connected with the story of the rape and are directed primarily against the inhabitants of Gibeah. From Chapter 20:12 on, criticism is directed against the tribe of Benjamin, who covered up for the people of Gibeah, and were thereby seen as lending their support to the outrage.[9]

The portrayal of the horribleness of what happened in Gibeah coupled with the Benjaminite response to the unanimous Israelite decision to seek justice indeed functions to provide a negative picture of the Benjaminites. The tribe of Benjamin is not interested in justice. They are interested more in protecting their own, however horrible the wrong deed perpetrated by the Benjaminites of Gibeah.

---

[9]Amit 345.

The authors of the Judges 19-21 pericope not only portray the Benjaminites as protecting the violators of justice against the collective Israel, they further cast a negative shadow on the Benjaminites by portraying them as a tribe which willingly kill other Israelites to protect the criminals. This stands in contrast to the collective Israelites, who are acting justly with divine sanction. In the following episode (Judges 20:17-48), in response to the Benjaminite mobilization of troops to protect the convicted criminals, an act amounting to a declaration of war, the Israelites mobilize troops of their own from every tribe, excepting that of Benjamin. The authors describe the collective Israel as the just ones who have the sanction of Yahweh. Israelites ask Yahweh's approval before fighting the Benjaminites (vv. 18, 23, 28). These verses – especially, verses twenty-three and twenty-eight – further indicate that the Israelites cared about the Benjaminites and were reluctant to fight them. In verse twenty-three, the Israelites wept before Yahweh, and ask if they should go up and fight against the Benjaminites, their "brother."

In verse twenty-eight, the Israelites ask if they should again fight the Benjaminites. This time, they even ask if they should cease the fight. The progression of the question formulas in verses eighteen, twenty-three, and twenty-eight, therefore, shows a gradual intensification of the Israelite reluctance to fight the Benjaminites. This concern for the Benjaminites that the Israelites exhibit in this episode is consistent with the next episode (Judges 21:1-24) in which Israelites go out of their way to save the tribe of Benjamin. In Judges 20:2-3, 6, the Israelites grieve for the defeated Benjaminites, who have the possibility of tribal extinction, and they try to find a solution to save them. Thus, the concern that Israelites show for the Benjaminites in conjunction with their consistent seeking of approval from Yahweh for the war portrays the Israelites as the executor of justice. In contrast, the authors of the Judges 19-21 pericope negatively characterize the tribe of Benjamin as one which did not care for justice, the good of fellow Israelites, but rather were merely interested in protecting their own even if it meant espousing injustice.

Even in the following episode (Judges 21:1-24), the authors of the Judges 19-21 pericope depict the Bejaminites negatively. Benjaminites are helpless losers who are completely at the mercy of the collective Israel. Israelites lament the possibility of the tribe of Benjamin being wiped out from Israel, since they have taken an oath collectively in Mizpah that they would not give their daughters in marriage to the remaining Benjaminites. The whole episode, therefore, is a story about how the Israelites try to go around this oath to save the tribe of Benjamin from extinction.

The first solution was to give four hundred virgins from Jabesh Gilead, whose lives are spared in the punishment-slaughter of the inhabitants for not attending the collective assembly at Mizpah. This is humiliating for the tribe of Benjamin since the women were from the tribe, which had received the death penalty for not being in the assembly of Yahweh. These women were portrayed as ones "worthy" for marriage with another group of transgressors, the Benjaminites. Humiliation of the tribe of Benjamin is carried out further in this episode. When the four hundred women from Jabesh Gilead are found to be insufficient in number for the Benjaminites, the elders of the collective Israelite assembly devise another plan to provide wives for the remaining Benjaminites. They instruct the Benjaminites to hide in the vineyards and then kidnap dancing women at the annual festival in Shiloh and then carry them off to the land of Benjaminites and form families through them. In this instance, the Benjaminites do not come off with a positive impression. The humiliation of the Benjaminites in this episode associated with their acquisition of wives to prevent extinction of their tribe is consistent with the overall negative portrayal of the Benjaminites in the Judges 19-21 pericope.

The negative portrayal of the Benjaminites in the Judges 19-21 pericope functions as an anti-Saul polemic and a pro-David polemic. The Benjaminites have participated in one of the most horrible atrocities in ancient Israel. Besides their participation in the ultimate act of inhospitality, the Benjaminites further committed wrong by extending their protecttion of the criminals to instigation of civil war that took many lives of the Israelites. In the aftermath of the war, Benjaminites are pitiable in that they acquire wives who are given pardon from death sentence in order to prevent the Benjaminite tribe from extinction. The Benjaminites also acquire wives through kidnapping. It is only because the elders of the Israelite assembly persuades the fathers of the kidnapped daughters to show mercy to the Benjaminites that the Benjaminites are allowed to build their tribe through them. This hardly seems like the kind of tribe from which the king of Israel should emerge.

This negative, anti-Saul pericope of Judges 19-21 functions to support the Royal Ideology. The House of David is the legitimate royal line for Israel. This is particularly evident in that it is the tribe of Judah that first goes to battle with Benjaminites in the war, and it is also they who lose their men valiantly in the first battle. Furthermore, it is Bethlehem, the place of David, that showed inordinate hospitality in the pericope. If Gibeah of the Benjaminites symbolizes inhospitality and injustice, Bethlehem of Judah represents a mode of hospitality. All these positive portrayals of Judah lead Barry G. Webb to comment: "Inasmuch as the monarchy is approved, it is the Davidic-Judahite monarchy which is in view."[10] Indeed, positive portrayal of Judahites and their city of Bethlehem and negative portrayal of Benjaminites and their city point toward pro-David and anti-Saul polemic.

Furthermore, a pro-Davidic idea exists in the implicit question: Would not the Levite and his concubine have been able to avoid this tragedy if they had remained in Jebus and spent the night there? The fact that Jebus could have been a possible city of refuge from injustice for the Levite and his concubine reminds the reader of David, who eventually conquered the city and made it an Israelite city. The text points out that Jebus is Jerusalem (Judges 19:10).

---

[10] Barry G. Webb, *The Book of the Judges: An Integrated Reading* (Sheffield: JSOT Press, 1987) 202.

The only reason that the Levite decide not to stay there is that it is not an Israelite city and he expects hospitality at an Israelite city. The reader, thus, comes to appreciate the significance of David's conquest of Jebus and making it Jerusalem, the city for Israelites.

The anti-Saul and pro-David polemic indeed exists in the final redacted composition of the Judges 19-21 pericope. Examination of the way in which the authors utilized their sources further highlights their anti-Saul and pro-Davidic propagandistic purpose. The most evident source is Genesis 19; the corresponding episode in the pericope is Judges 19:14-26.

From a literary perspective, there are too many similarities to disavow integral connection. In both the Judges episode and the Genesis portion, we have travelers who are provided lodging before they continue on the journey. Even the meeting place is similar. In Genesis, it is by the entrance of the city, and in Judges it is in the city square, which is right inside the city gates. Once in the house, the usual washing is mentioned before the consumption of food. In both accounts, the townsmen surround the house and demand for the male guest(s) to be brought out so that they might have sex with him (them). In both accounts, there is offering up of the daughter(s) of the host in the place of the guest(s). In both accounts, the men of the town would not listen, and the guest(s) intervene(s).

There are, however, visible differences. In the Genesis account the guests are angels, whereas in the Judges account the guests are humans – the

Levite from Ephraim and his concubine. In the Genesis account, Lot spots the angels by the city gate and persuades them to come and take advantage of his hospitality. In the Judges account, the Levite and his concubine are actively seeking hospitality. In the Genesis account, all of the men of the city are described as having surrounded the house, whereas in the Judges account some of the men of the city are described as having surrounded the house. In the Genesis account, two virgin daughters are offered up as substitutes; in the Judges account, one virgin daughter and the concubine of the guest are offered up by the host as substitutes. In the Genesis account, the guests intervene, causing the townsmen to become blind, with the conclusion of no harm done to the host or the guests. In the Judges account, the guest intervenes and offers up his own concubine, with the result that the concubine dies.

These differences, in fact, affirm the connectedness of the two episodes. The extant differences are only on the level of detail and not on the level of fundamental structure. Furthermore, differences are strategic. For example, from a literary perspective, it is significant that "all men" of the town in the Genesis account surround the house, whereas in the Judges account only "some" of the men of the town surround the house. This description is paralleled in their destruction. All of the men of Sodom are destroyed in God's punishment, whereas not all of the Benjaminites are destroyed in the war with rest of the Israelites. This is significant in indicating that all of the Sodomites were wicked, so God was justified in bring about total destruction. However, not all of the Benjaminites were wicked, so a total destruction was not necessary, even though partial destruction was necessary.

This is in tune with the perception of the Deuteronomists that transgression against God will be punished. In the Genesis passage, it was non-Israelites who transgressed against God and brought upon themselves God's punishment. In the Judges, it is Saul's tribe, the Benjaminites, who transgressed against God, and brought upon themselves the punishment.

What is particularly significant with the Judges passage over against the Genesis account is that the agent of punishment is the united Israelite tribes. This stands in contrast to the direct destruction of Sodom by God. This deviation from the punishment in the Genesis source by the author of the Judges 19-21 passage is intentional and meant to highlight the importance and strength of united Israel. The united Israel functions as Judge, Witness, and Executioner. This fits in well with the Deuteronomistic emphasis on political centralization and is in tune with the Deuteronomistic stress on human agency of divine punishment. The united Israel stands to deliver God's punishment to the Benjaminites. This portrayal in the Judges 19-21 pericope suits anti-Saul and pro-David propaganda.

It is not difficult to posit integral connectedness of the accounts from Genesis and Judges. What is difficult, however, is assessing the precise nature of the relationship between the two accounts. Niditch argues that the Judges episode preceded the Genesis account chronologically and might even have been a source for it. Besides considering the possibility that Genesis borrows from Judges, Niditch also allows the possibility for a borrowing of both Genesis and Judges from a common Israelite tale type.

Niditch, however, leans toward arguing for the primacy of the Judges pericope. Her argument is primarily based on her assertion that the episode fits well with rest of the narratives found in the pericope. In this light, events in Judges 19 provide an explanation for the war that follows in Judges 20, and are integral to the whole narrative. Thus, the motif of the homosexual rape as an epitome of anti-social, malevolent act of "inhospitality" is well-developed, and as such is used by the Genesis 19 episode as "an understandable choice as transition-marker for the destruction of Sodom."[11] And, Genesis 19:1-11 is a self-contained unit. Abraham's bartering episode (Genesis 18:23-33) right before it does not require this particular episode; Genesis 19:1-11 could, therefore, have had another story-pattern.

Theoretical underpinnings of Niditch's argument on primacy is based on the work of W. S. Towner. Since it plays such an important role in Niditch's theoretical presuppositions, I will quote her own correlation to Towner and conclusions regarding the two pericopes. Niditch writes:

> In his work on numerical pattern in rabbinical literature, W. S. Towner has essentially pointed to a *lectio difficilior* rule for literary traditions. The more

---
[11] Niditch 376.

complex, even the less neat the version of a tradition, often the earlier it is. The very brevity, comprehensibility, and plot-line simplicity of Gen 19:1-11 when compared with the complex patterns of event, the interlocking themes, and indeed the ambiguities of the account in Judges 19-20 point to the former's later status.[12]

This argument that longer, more complex text is earlier than a simpler, shorter version is by no means the majority consensus. In fact, it is the other way around. Scholars often take shorter, less complicated versions as preceding complex versions on the argument that the complex version represents development of the shorter version.

Thus, most scholars writing on the relationship between the Judges 19 and Genesis 19 episodes accept the primacy of the Genesis 19 version. One such scholar is J. Alberto Soggin. In fact, Soggin attributes complexity and differences in the Judges 19 episode to non-systematic use of the original source. Soggin writes: "The narrator has drawn considerably on Gen. 19 ... but without much coherence."[13] Furthermore, Soggin is in disagreement with Susan Niditch that "the threat of homosexual rape" is a central motif in the Judges episode. Niditch used the argument that because this motif is central to the narrative in that it even produces civil

---
[12]Niditch 376-377.
[13]J. Alberto Soggin, *Judges: A Commentary* (Philadelphia: The Westminster Press, 1981) 282.

war in Judges 20, this precedes the Genesis 19 version, which does not seem to require the particular homosexual rape theme for it to fit into the larger narrative context. Soggin argues that homosexual violence does not play a central role in the Judges passage. Soggin writes:

> The theme of homosexual violence, basic to Gen. 19 and therefore developed coherently ... from which only a miraculous intervention can rescue the destined victim, vv. 10f., appears only briefly in Judg. 19, but is irrelevant and does not produce any effect, given that the toughs are content to rape the woman (v. 25), leaving the levite and his servant alone.[14]

For Soggin, homosexual violence as a motif is much more central to the Genesis 19 episode than the Judges 19 episode, since initial homosexual violence was satiated by heterosexual violence in Judges. This textual reality weakens Niditch's argument that homosexual violence was developed in Judges as an ultimate anti-social, aggressive act of violence, and that the Genesis 19 merely used the motif. The actual violence in Judges was heterosexual violence, and that is what the Levite reports to the Israelite assembly. Based on this accusation, the Israelites rise up against the Benjaminites.

Thus, the main point of the Judges pericope is not a polemic against homosexual violence as the

---

[14]Soggin 282.

most aggressive form of inhospitality in Israel. Rather, primarily polemic is against the Benjaminites, the tribe of Saul. In keeping with the whole tenor of the Judges 19-21 pericope, the episode in Judges 19:14-26 is also an anti-Benjaminite and anti-Saul polemic.

The Genesis 19 source is utilized to facilitate this polemic. Amit writes regarding the use of Genesis 19 as a source by the authors of Judges 19: "The use of a similar dramatic outline and even similar wording directs every reader to feel the points of resemblance between the people of Gibeah and those of Sodom." [15] Thus, the authors of the Judges pericope utilized a pre-existent and well known source regarding wickedness of a people in order to portray the Benjaminites in the negative light. For the authors of Judges, however, homosexual violence was not of central concern. Rather, it was important for them to show that an actual violence was carried out in Gibeah by Benjaminites in distinction from Sodom, a wicked city, where violence was not carried out against the guests. Its primary purpose was an anti-Benjaminite polemic. Amit comments on the negative portrayal of the Benjaminites in Gibeah: "After the reader has grasped the general direction of the analogy, he discovers that the sin in Gibeah is painted as worse than that of the people of Sodom. In Sodom there was only a threat or attempt at rape (Gen 19:5-11), whereas in Gibeah a gang rape was carried out, resulting in the cruel death of the rape victim." [16] The Genesis 19 source, therefore,

---

[15] Amit 343.
[16] Amit 343.

functions to further highlight the anti-Benjaminite, anti-Saul polemic of the authors of the Judges 19-21 pericope.

Perceiving Judges 19-21 as an anti-Saul polemic raises the question of its place in biblical literature. Why is it at the end of the book of Judges? Is it meant to be a conclusion to the book of Judges? Or was it meant to be an introduction to the book of Samuel? Furthermore, if the Judges 19-21 pericope is a well-crafted literary piece with anti-Saul polemic, using even previous sources strategically to achieve this end, is it still possible that this literary composition points to a reality in ancient Israel? Or is it purely a literary creation?

Some scholars argue that the Judges 19-21 pericope was meant to be a conclusion to the book of Judges. One such scholar is Webb, who includes it as a part of the conclusion unit comprising Judges 17-21. Webb's primary argument hinges on the idea that the unit of Judges 17-21 functions as a part of the "bracketing" that complements the introduction to the book, found in Judges 1:1-3:6. Webb provides several examples of bracketing:

> The frequent references to Judah in these final chapters (17.7, 8, 9; 18.12, 20; 19.1, 2, 18) recalls the prominence given to Judah in 1.1-19; the characterization of Jebus/Jerusalem as 'a city of foreigners' in 19.10-12 recalls the note in 1.21 about the failure of the Benjaminites to expel the Jebusites; the weeping at Bethel in 20.18, 26

recalls the weeping at Bochim (=Bethel) in 2.1-5 ....[17]

For Webb, the introduction and the conclusion that bracket the book of Judges are integrally related to the literary unit that they enclose. Webb states: "The thesis which I wish to advance ... is that the book of Judges as a whole is ... a coherent literary work with thematic focus on the one hand and richness of meaning on the other."[18] For Webb, therefore, the whole book of Judges is a literary unity with the conclusion, including the Judges 19-21 pericope functioning as the other half of the bracket, along with the introductory section in the beginning.

    A. D. H. Mayes agrees with the concept that the introductory and the concluding sections form a sandwiching co-unit. Although Mayes agrees with Webb's delineation of the concluding unit (Judges 17-21), he does not agree with Webb on the chapters that are included in the introduction. Mayes includes Judges 1:1-2:5 within the introductory unit. Furthermore, Mayes disagrees with Webb by arguing that the introductory unit and the conclusion unit, while complementary, are later redactional interpolation on a continuous narrative that start from Joshua to Judges and Judges to Samuel.

    For instance, the internal Israelite struggles in Judges 17-21 stand in contrast to the Israelite fighting the external, foreign forces in Judges 2:11-16:31. Also, cultic lamentation and sacrifice are present in both the introduction and conclusion (Judges 2:4f.;

---

[17]Webb 197.
[18]Webb 76.

20:23, 26), in contrast to Judges 2:11-16:31. Most noticeable according to Mayes is the pro-monarchic bent of Judges 17-21, which situates the concluding section apart from the composition of the Judges 2:11-16:31 at a "post-deuteronomistic editing." Mayes argues that the conclusion material itself is from an early monarchic period when opposition for the monarchy was strong, but Mayes has difficulty understanding the motivation of the editor in including it with rest of the Judges corpus, except as a possible illustration of moral and spiritual decadence of Israel in the period of the Judges.[19]

Soggin differ from Mayes and Webb in that he does not see Judges 17-21 as a collective unit. Rather Soggin perceives Judges 17-18 as one unit and Judges 19-21 as another unit. Whereas Mayes and Webb argued that the whole unit of Judges 17-21 was pro-monarchical, Soggin argues that Judges 17-18 is pro-monarchical, but Judges 19-21 is not. Soggin comments regarding the Judges 19-21 pericope:

> Here the existence of an inter-tribal assembly is actually affirmed, an assembly which judges controversies that have broken out among the various members and whose decision appear to be binding on all, so much so that if necessary they are implemented by force of arms.[20]

---

[19] A. D. H. Mayes, *Judges* (Sheffield: JSOT Press, 1985) 13-16.
[20] Soggin 280.

Amit also perceives Judges 19-21 as providing a positive portrayal of the period. Amit writes: "Chapters 19-21 were added to the book artificially. .... The fact that these chapters do not contribute to the negative description of the period indicates that they are not part of the practical organization of Judges ...."[21] The logic that Soggin and Amit share is that Judges 19-21 is not explicitly pro-monarchic because the Judges 19-21 pericope describe effective political organization without a king.

Soggin notes that only the pro-monarchic formula in Judges 19:1 and Judges 21:25 are pro-monarchic elements within the Judges 19-21 pericope.[22] In agreement, Amit argues that the pro-monarchic formula, which she refers to as "the judgmental phrase," is meant to connect the Judges 19-21 pericope artificially to Judges 17-18.[23]

Where Soggin and Amit differ, however, is in Amit's perception that the Judges 19-21 pericope is heavy-laden with anti-Saul and pro-Davidic polemic. Thus, Amit is positing a form of Royal Ideology, minus the pro-monarchic factor. Indeed, anti-Saul and pro-David polemic characterizes the Judges 19-21 pericope. However, I would argue that Judges 19-21 represents a case for Royal Ideology, including the pro-monarchic factor. The Judges 19-21 pericope shows a glorification of political centralization, innate within Royal Ideology. The authors describe the politically centralized body of Israelites as inefficient and insufficient.

---

[21]Amit 342.
[22]Soggin 280.
[23]Amit 342.

Indeed, there is a glorification of political centralization. United Israel is valuable because it can dispense justice. On more than one occasion within the Judges 19-21 pericope, there is a description of Israelites acting as "one man" (Judges 20:1, 8) in order to dispense justice. However, the Judges 19-21 pericope portrays this politically centralized unity of Israelites as insufficient. The united Israelite tribes suffer severe casualties of war against one tribe, the Benjaminites, on first two campaigns.

On the first battle, there are twenty-two thousand dead on the Israelite side (Judges 20:21); on the second battle, there are eighteen thousand dead (Judges 20:24). Some scholars perceive the Israelite casualty as a form of divine punishment. Marais comments: "Not only Benjamin, but Israel too, received punishment in the course of this war. .... He used the war to chastise both parties."[24] And Webb writes: "Yahweh takes his place at the head of the assembly and distributes victory and defeat in such a way that the punishment of Benjamin by the other tribes is made the occasion for the whole of Israel to be chastised by Yahweh."[25] What was wrong with the Israelite unity? Can the sandwiching unit about the lack of a king in that period provide an explanation?

It is significant that the conclusion of the pericope includes the phrase, "everyone did what he saw fit," along with the phrase that in those days Israel had no king. This seems to fit well even with

---

[24] Jacobus Marais, *Representation in Old Testament Narrative Texts* (Leiden: Brill, 1998) 141.
[25] Webb 194.

the activity of the Israelites after the war. Instead of waiting for Yahweh's response and direction about preventing the possibility of the extinction of the tribe of Benjamin, the Judges 19-21 pericope describes the Israelites taking the matter into their own hands. The leaders of the Israelite unity devise various machinations to rectify this serious situation. The reader is left with the impression that a righteous king anointed by Yahweh would have acted differently in the situation described in the last episode of the Judges 19-21 pericope. This idea finds pithy expression in Judges 21:25.

The idea that a righteous king will support the proper worship of Yahweh is innate in Royal Ideology. Thus, the flip-side of Royal Ideology for the Deuteronomist is necessarily Zion Theology. In fact, various central ideas of the Zion Theology is evident in the Judges 19-21 pericope, such as the elevation of Yahweh and stressing the importance of observing oaths made to Yahweh.

In the Judges 19-21 pericope, Yahweh worship is elevated. Israelites offer burnt offerings and fellowship offerings to Yahweh in Bethel (Judges 20:26, 21:4). Furthermore, the united Israel consults Yahweh before every battle (Judges 20:18, 23, 28). Sacrifices are offered to no other gods nor are other gods consulted before war. Worship of Yahweh in Bethel is significant in that the authors of the Judges 19-21 pericope describe that the ark of the covenant was in Bethel "in those days" (Judges 20:27).

Furthermore, the authors of the Judges 19-21 pericope seem to provide an excuse for the worship of Yahweh in Bethel and not in Jerusalem. Judges

19:10-12 reminds the reader that Jerusalem was still "Jebus" in the days of the pericope when the Israelites worshipped Yahweh in Bethel. In verse eleven, the servant of the Levite describes Jebus as the city of Jebusites. Furthermore, in verse twelve, the Levite refuses to stay in Jebus even though his servant wants to, because it is an "alien city" and the people are not Israelites. Judges 19:10-12, therefore, provides justification for the worship of Yahweh in Bethel in the context of the Judges story. Thus, Zion Theology is upheld. Yahweh must be worshipped and him alone, but Yahweh could not be worshipped in Jerusalem as is proper because Jerusalem was not yet an Israelite city in the days of the story in the Judges 19-21 pericope.

Besides this elevation of Yahweh worship, oaths made to Yahweh receive special attention in the Judges 19-21 pericope as one that must not be broken, but rather kept. The Judges 19-21 pericope, therefore, describes Israelites' extended efforts not to break the oaths, but rather go around the oaths made to Yahweh. However, the portrayal of the Israelite unity outsmarting the oath made to Yahweh privileges political expediency. Furthermore, this seems to point toward the idea that everyone did what was fit in his eyes because there was no king.

There are two oaths. One oath is that any tribe that does not attend the assembly of Israel in Mizpah after the defeat of the Benjaminites will be put to death (Judges 21:5). No one from Jabesh Gilead attended, so the Israelite unity decides to put them to death. Oath made to God is sacred and must be kept in Deuteronomistic ideology. However, the united Israelite tribes spare the virgin women of Jabesh Gilead because these women serve the Israelite unity's political purpose of providing wives for the remaining wife-less men of the tribe of Benjamin.

Another oath is not to give any of the daughters to the men from the tribe of Benjamin who are left over after the war (Judges 21:1). After the oath is made to Yahweh, members of the Israelite unity lament because they regret having made the oath and a tribe of Israel might cease to be. Instead of waiting for Yahweh's response to the solution, the Israelite unity takes matters into their hand and devises plans to go around the oath. First, they offer up virgin women from Jabesh Gilead to Benjaminite men. But four hundred women from Jabesh Gilead prove to be insufficient in number. Thus, Israelites find another way around the oath. They tell the Benjaminites to kidnap women at the annual festival at Shiloh and carry them off as wives into their land. Since kidnap is involved, this would not necessitate the breaking of the oath that no Israelite will give his daughter to a Benjaminite. The Israelite leadership anticipate complaints from the fathers of the kidnapped daughters and, therefore, devises a plan to persuade them to do a favor and let the matter slide. They planned also to assure the fathers of their innocence vis-á-vis oath made to God, since the daughters were kidnapped and not given by their fathers. The whole event seems unjust for the kidnapped women and their fathers.

The reader is referred to the conclusion in Judges 21:25 that Israel had no king, so it did what it wanted. The pro-monarchic formula provides criticism not only of the Benjaminites who participated in wrong perpetrated by the Benjaminite men of Gibeah, but also of the Israelite unity, which also practiced unjust policies. Remnant in the criticism is the idea that a proper Yahweh-fearing king of Israel would not have allowed all this to happen.

The Judges 19-21 pericope, therefore, provides an ideological argument for the value of a proper king. Anti-Benjaminite and pro-Judahite polemic in the text points toward favoring of David (and his line) as the proper king and functions to discourage loyalty to Saul and his line. Therefore, Royal Ideology reigns supreme in the pericope. Zion Theology, a flip-side of Royal Ideology also exerts itself in the Judges 19-21 pericope.

And Zion Theology functions strategically to prop up Royal Ideology. In a sense, the support of Royal Ideology is necessarily a support of Zion Theology.

The Dueteronomistic ideologies of Royal Ideology and Zion Theology function as ideological texts in the Judges 19-21. Are there any other prominent ideological texts in the pericope? Before answering this question, a treatment of the idea of "text" would be important.

What do I mean by text? By text, I refer to any conceptual reality. Practically, anything can be a text. Documents are written texts. Archaeological finds are material texts. An idea is an ideological text. Even genre could be a text. What is the significance of deconstructing each element into such vague conceptual reality? It allows for comparisons across ordinarily delineated boundaries. Not only are comparisons possible, but also cohesion of separate texts into coherent unit are achievable along the same lines that written texts are combined as cohesive argument to support an idea.

To provide an example of this, I would like to refer to modern academic discourse on politics and religion in the ancient world. Often, academic discourse separates and distinguishes these two elements in the ancient world. Even from an academic disciplinary perspective, political science and religion are differentiated by separate departments. Some might possibly see Politics as the body and Religion as the soul. Such dichotomization is, in part, a product of the Cartesian model that has plagued modern scholarship. In the ancient world, such dichotomized way of looking at the world did not exist. Religion and Politics were inevitably intertwined. However, it would be unfair to do away with the contributions of a focused inquiry that isolates a factor within a reality. If the pitfalls of dichotomization could be rectified, the gains of individualized study will contribute to the holistic understanding of a reality. Thus, Politics and Religion are different texts that work together towards better understanding of one reality. It is important to note, however, they are qualitatively equivalent as texts; one does not have a predominance of one over the other for understanding reality, as might be the case in the Cartesian model of body versus soul.

To provide a tangible example, I would like to refer to a painting that depicts a custom, like the Taurobolium, and a written document from an ancient writer describing the same practice. The written text as well as the picture text provides a picture into the historical phenomenon of Taurobolium. In the qualitative sense, there is no reason why Religion and Politics could not function as two separate texts that describe the same phenomenon. For instance, ancient kingship can be described in terms of Religion and also in terms of Politics, but they describe the same reality. Thus, treating Religion and Politics as texts allows these two disciplines to be complementary. And since "text" is a neutral entity, this allows a bilateral comparison.

In line with this presentation of "text," I would like to point out that Royal Ideology and Zion Theology are texts – ideological texts. They are more specific than the generic "Politics" and "Religion." But they function in the same way as the theoretical situation described above in that they both work together as separate texts on equal level to describe the same reality. We have seen an imbalanced presentation of the reality of the Judges 19-21 pericope, when Zion Theology, an important Deuteronomistic idea and often referred to as the flip-side of the Royal Ideology, was ignored in the examination of the pericope.

Studying just the Royal Ideology or just the Zion Theology within the Judges 19-21 pericope is not an unproductive exercise. It contributes to a better understanding of an aspect of the reality of the pericope. However, taking two central ideological texts related to the pericope provides a fuller, and even more accurate, understanding of the reality of the pericope.

I would argue that Social Justice is a text for the Deuteronomist in the same extent that Royal Ideology or Zion Theology is. For the sake of this paper, it would be useful to restate the previous sentence. Social Justice is separate but complementting text in the Judges 19-21 pericope as Royal Ideology and Zion Theology. And Social Justice as an ideological text plays a central role in the pericope.

An added benefit of studying Social Justice as a text is allowing the modern student of ancient Israel to examine through separate categorization its intrinsic worth in the context of the ancient Israelite society. At the same time, since "text" is the most deconstructed theoretical construct, it would allow the closest possible approximation to the actual function of social justice in ancient Israelite society by allowing it to work conjunctively with other "texts" in ancient Israel. To expand on this idea, social justice was not necessarily perceived as a separate issue from Religion or Politics. Just as the study of Religion and Politics − or Zion Theology and Royal Ideology − as separate texts does not negate their intrinsic connectedness to each other in ancient society, the study of Social Justice as a separate text does not negate its intrinsic connectedness to other texts in ancient Israel. In this regard, social justice will receive its due careful attention, while providing another element in academic discourse for accurate perception of the reality of the Judges 19-21 pericope.

Now, the important question is − how do we isolate Social Justice as a text? It is my argument that Social Justice as a text is isolatable in Judges 19-

21, especially in the portion in which the Deuteronomistic school utilizes and reshapes the Genesis 19 episode. Particularly useful in isolating the Social Justice text is the work of Soggin. Although Soggin does not use the term "social justice," his argument that "high ethical standard" is a unifying factor of the Judges 19-21 pericope is particularly helpful in laying the ground work for a discussion of social justice as a text. Thus, I will provide a sizable portion of Soggin's writing on this regard. Soggin writes:

> The criterion which governed this unification by the redactors seems to be the declaration which we find repeated, "Has such a thing ever happened from the time when the Israelites came out of Egypt to the present day...?" (19.30; 20.6b-7). This seems to be the theme of the redactors: certain things should not happen in Israel because they are incompatible with the concept of the people of God which the redactors proclaim. The redactors therefore propose to their hearers and readers a very high ethical standard: certain things may happen among other people, but they must not come about in Israel; where they do come about all the same, the event suspends every criterion of tribal solidarity: the guilty ones must be

handed over to the institutions responsible for the punishment which they deserve. And it is precisely this consideration which is the connecting link between the narrative of the levite and that of the war against Benjamin.[26]

Here, Soggin provides some useful fields of reference. The story recounting the punishment of Benjaminites is linked to the story of the Levite and his concubine by the crime that is done in Gibeah. The message is that on the basis of high ethical standard reserved for Israelites, the redactor is showing that violators of this ethical standard must be punished. For Soggin, the phrase that a horrible thing like this has not happened since the Israelites left Egypt connects the two sections and points to the redactor's implicit assertion that it should not happen.

Although Soggin's discussion of "high ethical standard" is useful as an initial starting point, lack of precise definition and detail leave his analysis only in the initial stages. What does "high ethical standard" mean? Would it be required to point to gang rape and murder as a crime? Furthermore, Soggin does not explain in clear terms what wrong was committed. Is it the gang rape of the concubine? Is it murder? Is it inhospitable treatment?

It is my contention that "social justice" rather than "high ethical standard" would be a better term to describe the concern of the authors of the Judges 19-21 pericope. In fact, Social Justice as a text is pervasive in the Judges 19-21 pericope. This is most

---

[26]Soggin 301.

evident in the way Judges 19 reshapes the Genesis 19 source and the implication of the variation for the whole Judges 19-21 pericope. One of the primary differences is the conclusion. In the Genesis 19 episode, the angels intervene and neither the guests nor anyone from the host family are injured. In the Judges 19 episode, the concubine of the Levite is offered up to the mob and is gang raped and dies as the result. What is significant is that the host saw liberty to offer up the Levite's concubine to the mob.

The Levite's concubine was also a guest of the host along with the Levite. The fact that the host felt at liberty to offer her up to the mob shows the perceived low status of the concubine. Not only is the concubine not bound by the guest-host hospitality rule, she is expandable. The Levite is not even consulted; it is expected by the host that the Levite would agree to such an arrangement.

This expectation is verified in the following action of the Levite. The Levite pushes his concubine out to the mob. The fact that he expects her to meet her death is evident in his reaction the following morning. The Levite sees his concubine lying on the doorsteps, puts her on the donkey, when she does not respond to his command to get up. Furthermore, the fact that the Levite expected his concubine to meet her death is affirmed in the Levite's speech to the Israelite assembly. The Levite argues that the men of Gibeah wanted to kill him (Judges 20:5). In the account in Judges 19, the men of Gibeah only demanded to have sex with him.

The understanding here is that if the mob had their way with the Levite, he would have ended up dead just like his concubine. Knowing that his concubine would meet her death, the Levite pushed her out into the mob. This indicates the concubine's value for the Levite. For the Levite as well, she is expandable.

The idea that the concubine in her status is expandable is not a new motif. Hagar, who became Abraham's concubine, is portrayed as expandable. When Sarah complained to Abraham, Abraham allowed her to do whatever she wanted to her. There were no limits. Sarah oppressed her so much that Hagar fled into the desert (Genesis 16:5-6). A nearly certain death is preferred over Sarah's affliction. Indeed, Hagar is saved only by Yahweh's intervention. Later in the patriarchal narratives, Hagar, along with Ishmael, is sent out from the Abraham's camp toward the wilderness at the desire of Sarah (Genesis 21:10, 14). Hagar, Abraham's concubine, is portrayed as expandable. This expandability even seems to have divine sanction, as Yahweh tells Abraham to do as Sarah wishes (Genesis 21:12). At no point are Abraham and Sarah implicated for basically sending Hagar to a possible death in the wilderness.

In contrast, the authors of the Judges 19-21 pericope go out of their way to show that a concubine is not expandable. In fact, as the result of what happened to the concubine, Israelite tribes gather in an assembly. After gathering as the result of receiving pieces of the concubine's body, the united Israelites hear out the Levite. After learning what happened – gang rape of the concubine and her subsequent death – all of Israel decide to seek justice against the perpetrators, which results in a war against Benjaminites. As the result of one murder of a concubine, a whole tribe of Benjamin almost becomes extinct. The possible extinction of the tribe of Benjamin is mentioned several times in the pericope and the united Israel is portrayed as utilizing various machinations to save them. The gang rape and murder of the concubine was a serious matter.

In fact, one can argue that the whole Judges 19-21 pericope structurally centers around the crime against the concubine. It is the literary climax. The previous episode of the Levite pursuing his concubine to Bethlehem in Judah leads up to the scene of ultimate inhospitality in Gibeah. Even the inhospitality that the Levite and his concubine receive sitting by the city square is foreboding. The old man from Ephraim who invites them into his home tells the Levite and his concubine not to spend the night at the square (Judges 19:20). This further adds to the foreboding. Then, the crime happens. The episodes following the crime are direct results of the crime. Thus, the crime – the rape and murder of the concubine – is the climax of the whole pericope.

The question rises – why the concubine? Why is she the victim? It is precisely because her social status within the ancient Israelite society is negligible that she is chosen as an ideal victim to propound social justice issues. The gargantuan nature of the consequence of the crime done against the concubine points to the authors' concerns for the socially insignificant. Even one of the socially least significant has a value.

Wrong done against her is a wrong done against Yahweh that needs to be punished. To satisfy social justice, it is worthy for the whole Israelites to be mobilized. Not only that, one life of the concubine is significant enough to lose the twenty-two thousand Israelite lives in the first battle and eighteen thousand Israelite lives in the second battle. Social justice is that important.

This valuing of a concubine's social value and stressing the importance of seeking social justice for the wrong done against her along with the phrase that nothing terrible as this has been done in Israel since Israelites left Egypt is reminiscent of the formula employed by the Deuteronomists – "Remember that you were once slaves in Egypt" – which is found throughout the book of Deuteronomy. For instance, Deuteronomy 24:17-18 states: "You shall not subvert the rights of the stranger or the fatherless; you shall not take a widow's garment in pawn. Remember that you were a slave in Egypt and that the LORD your God redeemed you from there; therefore do I enjoin you to observe this commandment" (New JPS). Such language espousing social justice for the underprivileged, the outsider, is employed here in the Judges 19-21 pericope. In the days in Egypt such acts of injustice might have happened. After all, slaves suffered a lot at the hands of the oppressors. But since the exodus from Egypt, such oppression has not happened.

Now that it happened, the implication is that the social injustice must be rectified. And indeed, a significant portion of the Judges 19-21 pericope describes an effort to right this social injustice by punishing the perpetrators and those who were protecting the perpetrators.

The concern for the oppressed is in tune with the general concern that the Deuteronomists show to the oppressed. Although for the purpose of this paper, it is too extensive of an exercise to give this a fair treatment, it is important to point out that social justice is a very important concern to the Deuteronomists, as much as Royal Ideology and Zion Theology are. Social Justice as a text emerge throughout the Deuteronomistic literature. It may be worthwhile to give social justice a comprehensive treatment in the future.

A Critical and Theoretical Conceptualization of Ritual Studies and Its Application in the Ancient Roman World[1]

Nancy Jay's work, *Throughout Your Generations Forever: Sacrifice, Religion, and Paternity*, discusses ritual in the context of sociology and social theory of religion. For Jay's study, ritual is a map into social dynamics and reality that points toward greater patterns of social practices. One can see an example of this particularly in the chapter entitled, "The Logic of Sacrifice." Jay writes: "Sacrifice joins people together in community and, conversely, it separates them from defilement, disease, and other dangers. This opposition of joining and separating is so widespread that one of the clearest indications that a ritual killing is properly sacrifice is that it is part of a religious system of this kind."[2]

In light of this idea that runs throughout her book, Nancy Jay employs a descriptive study with an analysis of social context and social content. Particularly helpful is Jay's awareness of patriarchal forms that are perpetuated by certain ritual practices. In light of this awareness, one sees an interpretive method that is enlightening in understanding certain aspect of social reality.

---

[1] This paper was written in the context of the Ph.D. program in Judaic Studies at Brown University in 1998.
[2] Nancy Jay, *Throughout Your Generations Forever: Sacrifice, Religion, and Paternity* (Chicago and London: The University of Chicago Press, 1992) 17.

Further helpful is Nancy Jay's exposition of these ideas by using particular examples from various ritual practices in specific contexts. For instance, Nancy Jay points out that women are often excluded from sacrifice in cultures – she refers to the Nuer religion as an example – and indicates that such sacrificial mores is indicative of social mores and reality; namely, emphasis on paternity.[3]

Thus, in the context of a larger study of religions, Jay contributes particularly to the epistemological process in the study of ritual. How does one know what one knows? For her, the logic of ritual practice is epistemological reality for the logic of society.

Jay's study provides very helpful insight into the connection between religious ritual and society but is somewhat limited in studying religious ritual as one of the competing elements in society that affect it. Sometimes rituals continue in certain ways, as a matter of seasoned practice, whereas various other institutions in society may undergo change. Thus, political institutions, various educational institutions, the social unit of "family" can experience developmental manifestations that may not totally be reflected in the religious institution or ritual (loosely defined). Yet, this does not deny the interrelatedness of various forms and developments within various elements in society. Sometimes, social developments precede religious developments and, other times, vice versa. And, yet, other times, they may function together.

---

[3] Jay 36.

Catherine Bell's theoretical exposition on the concept of "ritualization" in her book, *Ritual Theory, Ritual Practice*, takes into consideration limiting scope of the emphasis on understanding society exclusively from religious rituals. Bell sees a fundamental problem of limit associated with the word "ritual," but still prefers a theoretical framework that utilizes contribution of previous studies on ritual, rather than replacing ritual studies with a totally new methodology.[4] Thus, Bell concentrates on the process by which a ritual becomes a ritual. Bell writes: "When analyzed as ritualization, acting ritually emerges as a particular cultural strategy of differentiation linked to particular social effects and rooted in a distinctive interplay of a socialized body and the environment it structures."[5] This emphasis on process rather than form allows greater flexibility in studying non-religious activities also as ritualizations, or rituals.

Indeed Bell's theory of ritualization adds greater depth to Jay's theory of ritual. Yet, there are limits to Bell's theory, especially in studying ancient religions and ancient societies, which are fixed in time in the past. In this light, I would like to propose my own theoretical model for studying ritual with the purpose of understanding its implication in and for the society, in which it is found. My theoretical model takes the form of an atom, and I will expand on it with accompanying examples, as they will help in the clarification of the theory.

---

[4] Catherine Bell, *Ritual Theory, Ritual Practice* (New York: Oxford University Press, 1992) 4.
[5] Bell 7-8.

The starting point for my theoretical study of ritual in the context of ancient religions and ancient society takes into consideration the question of the place of ritual. Ritual studies often start from religion and then proceed further analysis into the society and the social context. Conceptually, religious rituals, such as sacrifice, function as the nucleus of an atom, and the atom represents the society.

Although seeing the value of studying religious rituals for understanding society, I would like to assert that, in theory, ritual should be divested of its innately religious content to allow further versatility to ritual studies. This is not to say that many rituals are not religious; often, rituals are religious. However, one should allow for social rituals, educational rituals, and so on. Seeing ritual as encompassing all aspects of society, including religious, social, and educational, will be helpful in assessing the social reality from a more complex angle.

Thus, my model has a ritual as a nucleus, but the ritual does not have to be of a particular kind; the "nucleus ritual" can be social, religious, educational, etc. In keeping with the structural model of the atom, there are rituals that represent electrons, which are an integral part of the atom, revolving around the nucleus ritual, and which give the atom its character. All this is in the context of the atom, which represents the society.

To give a practical example of my model, let us consider the ancient Roman world. At the time of Augustus, there was the offering of sacrifices for the emperor's sake to gods and "giving" of political honors to Augustus. Now, in my model, one should study different rituals – that is, sacrifice and paying political homage to Augustus – as equally important elements for understanding the society. Yet, often this is impractical from an academic point of view. Thus, one would focus on sacrifice or paying homage to Augustus as the nucleus ritual.

The study of "nucleus ritual" will have its own implications. For instance, studying sacrifice will necessitate a contextual diachronic study of the particular sacrifice in the context of sacrifice ritual tradition. Thus, for example, one would ask such a question regarding the sacrifice performed at that particular time: Is it indicative of sacrifice that is given as an appeasement of God or wish for blessing? These two elements, though seemingly equal, are not and provide particular understanding of the "nucleus ritual" itself and will have an implication for understanding the ritual in the context of other rituals ("electron rituals") and of the society as well ("the atom").

If one were to make giving of honor to Augustus as the "nucleus ritual," one would have to see this in the context of its own diachronic historical tradition. Thus, one would ask the question, did the Romans normally give honors to their emperor? This question, of course, is difficult to answer for any student of Roman history, since the concept of the emperor was a recent phenomena in ancient Rome by the time of Augustus. Roman history entered the period of the "Empire" with Augustus, and before that we have the Roman Republic.

One can start with Julius Caesar as a possible comparative model. But one other example is hardly enough to provide a normative model of a "nucleus ritual" or a proper understanding of it. Then, one is faced with the question, is it possible to compare a political reality ("the emperor") with a similar institution in the Roman Republic, such as "dictator"? Difficulty presents itself in comparing an element in one institution that came to be vested with religious and political functions – such as the emperor, especially by the time of Augustus[6] – with the institution of the dictator which was primarily a political-military one.

---

[6] In 12 BC, Augustus became *pontifex maximus*, which was the highest religious office in Rome. Cassius Dio recounts: "When Lepidus died, Augustus was appointed high priest and the Senate wished on this account to vote him other honours, but he replied that he would accept none of them; when the senators pressed him, he rose and left the chamber" (*The Roman History*, 54.27). Concerning the political significance of the addition of the highest religious office in the person of Augustus, Caston Boissier writes: "Une seule fonction lui manquait pour être le chef de la religion romaine, celle de grand pontife: Il l'attendit longtemps, et, ce qui lui fait honneur, il eut la patience de l'attendre" (Gaston Boissier, *La Religion Romaine d'Auguste aux Antonins* {Paris: Librairie Hachette, 1874} 93). Furthermore, the office of the pontifex maximus had high political manipulation potential. Liebeschuetz explains: "So the Roman calendar, supervised by the *pontifices* could and did manipulate the insertion of intercalary months in such a way as to provide more or less time for legislation, or to extend or reduce the tenure of a particular office holder, or the length of a particular public contract" (J. H. W. G. Liebeschuetz, *Continuity and Change in Roman Religion* {Oxford: Oxford University Press, 1979} 2).

This discussion highlights the particular difficulty of doing ritual studies (especially if one wants to provide a normalizing principle of sorts). For, even an initial study of the nucleus ritual entails proper assessment of the ritual in its own right and in its own diachronic context. This study is made difficult by the reality of the changing historical environment. To take a snap shot picture of the nucleus ritual (one event) cannot be used as a normalizing element to make a statement about a society with any certainty.

Yet, students of ritual studies have to find a way of doing nucleus ritual studies. And it is my thinking that this is possible to the extent that we can learn something helpful about the nucleus ritual and also about the society at large with the result that we can say something concrete about both the ritual and society.

Thus, one can study the sacrifices or the giving of honor to Augustus in its own diachronic context, as a starting point. But one must keep in mind that the study of one element as a "nucleus ritual" does not exclude one's study of the other element.

Although our working term is "electron ritual," I would like to forward that it is equally important to devote rigorous study to the second ritual. This is particularly important in light of the simultaneous nature of both rituals. They were done at the same time by the same group of people.

This study, done in the context of the social environment, will provide one with a forwardable statement of social reality. Thus, I am supporting a form of ethnographic study done with a diachronic emphasis and with a sensitivity to dynamics of rituals as they function in society even outside what one would usually call "the religious."

It is somewhat unfortunate that the human was identified as "Homo religiosus." This was helpful in the context of academic studies at the time of its inception, but it would be a shame if the emphasis on humans as innately religious beings holds the scholar back from a balanced study of the human experience and of society at large. Human beings experience many things in life. Religion is only one part of the human experience, however important that may be.

The idea that traditional societies were innately religious can be seen, in part, as a product of such past inquiry. Even studying "traditional" societies, one would benefit from divestiture of religion as the primary understanding of an individual, her society, or religion. Ritual studies as well as religious studies will continue to benefit from the growing emphasis toward sociological, anthropological, social historical emphasis in the study of religion and society.

Thus, in Ancient Rome *Lex Julia de maritandis ordinibus* and *Lex Julia de adulteriis* of Augustus were not purely religious laws to maintain Roman morality. Sir Ronald Syme perceived these as Augustus' efforts for political stability in the form of patronage: "The aim of the new code was no less than this, to bring the family under the protection of the State...."[7] Also, Virgil's writings about *virtus* and *pietas* were not merely to spur the populace to lofty ideals, nor was Horace's evoking of Republican ideals of the rugged farmer purely for bringing back traditionalism. Syme writes:

> If the citizen refused to fight, the city would perish at the hands of its enemies – or its mercenaries. Augustus appealed to the virtues of a warrior race. .... The ideal of virtue and valour was not Roman only, but Italian, ingrained in the Sabines of old and in Etruria, when Etruria was martial. .... In the exaltation of 'Itala virtus' Rome magnified her valour, for Rome had prevailed over Italy.[8]

Thus, even literature evoking virtue, written under Augustus' patronage, can be seen as a part of his efforts for political stability after his victory at Actium. Historical interpretation of religion and examination of seeming efforts at virtue in light of social and political developments are helpful in formulating a model for ritual studies. But I believe that ritual studies have a lot to contribute to ancient studies as well. It is this very corroborative study that will continue to spur academic inquiry.

With this thought, I will focus on Augustus in an effort to provide a possible working model for

---

[7]Ronald Syme, *The Roman Revolution* (Oxford: Oxford University Press, 1939) 444.
[8]Syme 448-449.

ritual studies. I prefer to make granting of political honors as the nucleus ritual. My decision hinges on the fact that granting of honors in ancient Rome was always seen as a form of social stabilization. This held true for the Empire as well as for the Republic. Thus, returning military leader was granted a dictatorial welcome with laurel leaves and the whole populace cheering on. The leader brought peace and victory (= prosperity in the ancient world); thus, the leader was rewarded. Titles continued to be heaped upon the leader with further prosperity. This rewarding of titles was as much a sign of appreciation as a desire for continuance of such prosperity. This Republican practice continued on in Caesar's time. By the time of Augustus, this practice (ritual practice) was well in place. Thus, in light of this diachronic reality, one understands granting of honors to Augustus as a ritual that Romans innately believed to be important for the bringing about of prosperity. Now, the nucleus ritual is crudely provided.

Regarding sacrifices to gods, this electron ritual can also be seen as an effort to maintain prosperity and peace. But it would be beneficial to see all this in light of the development within the religious tradition in which perception of gods has gone through much diachronic development. There is Euhemerism, where gods were seen as great human being that lived before and gained status as gods. Heritage such as this brought about a greater realization in the Roman society of import of human agency. There are other ideas shared by Greeks and Romans that brought about a movement toward human agency.

Take the Greek philosophical schools, for instance. There was a fragmentation of philosophy in the Hellenistic period. Traditionally "Platonic" ideas found development in Middle Platonism and various philosophical schools that competed with each other for students, followers, and ideas. Stoicism, Cynicism, Epicureanism – all of them by their sheer existence and disagreement in ideas (Stoicism is often described as pantheistic and Epicureanism is thought of as atheistic) provided an intellectual realization for the value of human agency.

Furthermore, one cannot discount other movements that existed within the Roman Empire and the Roman provinces. There were holy men movements throughout the empire. There were healers, such as Honi the Circle Drawer and Hanina ben Dosa, who gained prominence. Even in the cult of Aesculus, it was less divine agency and more human agency that gained prominence in the realization of healing. Other mystery religions, such as the cult of Isis and Orpheus, came to value human agency. They emphasized reactualization and "acting out" of divine stories as having value.

Thus, one sees Taurobolium – actualization of sacred myth by ritual baptism, which Roman soldiers underwent – as a value. The fact that Roman soldiers were "encouraged" to participate in these mystery rituals before going to battle is indicative of the reality of greater reliance in human agency. It was the Roman army that will win the war, not the gods. Thus, they will participate in the rituals themselves, rather than sacrifice to traditional gods for their victory. In every fabric of Roman society, greater emphasis on the human agency was felt.

Now, it becomes clear why sacrifice to gods is placed under "electron ritual" and granting of honor to Augustus would be seen as a "nucleus ritual." Granting of honor to a human leader for national prosperity has been in practice and was gaining ascendancy at the time of Augustus in the context of diachronic development within the political tradition of granting of honors as well as within the diachronic development within the Roman religion in which sacrifice gradually came to take back seat to mystery religions, Graeco-Roman philosophical schools, and other elements that emphasized human agency.

One notices that I have brought in historical developments in the Roman provinces in discussion. I would forward that this is relevant especially at the time of Augustus. We remember that at the time of the Triumvirate, various leaders of Rome vied for power by means of enlisting allies from the peripheries of its empire as well as those of the provinces. We even know the battle of Actium, which resulted in the death of the Egyptian empress Cleopatra and of Marcus Anthony, who died together as lovers and co-regents of Egypt. There was active involvement of Rome in its provinces (and even in its peripheries).

Furthermore, we remember the conscription policies under Julius Caesar. Shortage of army produced greater recruitment of soldiers from outside Rome. Those in the provinces saw greater extension of rights as Roman citizens. And Roman soldiers stationed in provinces intermarried with women from the provinces.

Furthermore, Julius Caesar's Pax Romana and all the road work throughout his empire continued under Augustus's Pax Augustana. Greater developments in trade, exchange of ideas, travel of people within the Roman Empire had a way of unifying the Roman Empire to the extent that Rome was integrally connected to developments and experiences of those in its provinces. In sum, my discussion of the provinces is, therefore, legitimated historically.

Now, that we have discussed nucleus ritual and an electron ritual in brief. Next methodological step is to identify other electrons. Will this atom be a helium or gold? Other possible electrons can be seen as rituals in education, such as rhetoric or writing/ literature. What "rituals" can be identified in rhetoric, and how do they provide constructive understanding of the whole picture?

For one, the increase in the emphasis of rhetoric as a field of study and social art is significant in the study of ritual; for, on a basic level, ritual of rhetoric communication is indicative of emphasis on human agency. Also, how about letter writing? The ritual of letter writing itself saw a diachronic development. In the ancient Near East, letters were written back and forth primarily by chief political leaders. The concept and ritual practice of letter writing between everyday ordinary people must be seen in its diachronic context in which the Roman philosophical concepts of friendship and patronage, necessitated such rituals. Why were friendships elevated to the level of *arete*? This, on a simple level, can be seen as emphasis on human agency. The concept of patronage involved not only writing letters, but can even be seen in a larger context as an "electron ritual" in its own right.

One can even argue that Augustus can be seen as a patron to the Roman people and that their granting him honor can be seen on one level as a ritual practice of patronage. After all, one remembers that Augustus' patron deity was made official patron deity of Rome. Although a historian would have to argue on the basis of this for Augustus' efforts at deification, one can easily see that the ritual practice of patronage places Augustus in a semiotic relationship with the Roman people. As was the case with patron deities, Augustus' patron deity represented Augustus (and actually was the embodiment of Augustus and his family). For Romans to have Augustus's patron deity as their official patron god was tantamount to placing themselves in a patron-client relationship with Augustus. Romans knew this.

Another electron ritual can be seen as the development in the Roman *familia*. We know that the Roman family was increasingly becoming important in Augustus' time. There was much legislation of family laws. There was increased granting of land rights to those who had previously been deprived of it, such as women. There were legislations that women with certain numbers of children will be granted inheritance rights/land rights. What do all these historical data mean?

In the context of ritual studies, certain family rituals can be identified. It is, to be sure, a little bit difficult to identify rituals in the context of the broad concept of the family. But this is not to say that this cannot be done. One has to realize that much of ritual studies to this point has focused on "religious" rituals, and particularly on the concept of sacrifice. Thus, discussing sacrifice as ritual seems like a normative discussion, whereas the use of the term to discuss family or family practices may sound foreign. It is merely a matter of topos, or academic language. And one knows that academic language develops and is in flux. Especially in the context of growing interdisciplinary studies, it is important to explore new ways of discussion.

One proposal that I have for discussing the family and family practices as ritual is to approach them from the angle of studying them in the context-framework of ritual. What do I mean? One discusses sacrifice as something that is done by someone/group to someone/group for something with certain results. Often ritual is marked by its frequency and context/purpose. One can also approach the family or family practices with this model. Although it will take more thinking to develop this methodologically and practically, I believe that it is possible. Bell's understanding of "ritualization" will be particularly helpful in this regard.

Now, there can be more electron rituals to consider, but I will stop here for now, since this is only a preliminary thinking on the issue. I will move on to the concept of the context of the atom. Although some scientists have argued once that the nucleus and electron exist in a vacuum and form what we know as the atom, scientists have come to realize that there may be other factors to be considered –

such as possible friction and other matters that does not exist within the simple model of the atom that was expounded on before.

Whatever the developments are in the area of science, it is important to keep in mind that the nucleus ritual and electron rituals in our model of ritual studies exist in a larger socio-historical context of the atom. One may be aware that the much ground would be covered in a proper study of nucleus ritual and electron rituals in the way of diachronic studies. Yet, synchronic studies are indispensable in the context of any fruitful historical study. And it is this synchronic study that the context of the atom in our model of ritual studies provides. Not, only is the step of comparing and relating events and realities from nucleus ritual and electronic rituals important at this stage from a methodological point of view, formulating constructive statements or assertion for discussion would be actualized at this step. Thus, factors to be considered are questions such as: what are some existent gaps in the discussion that are needed to provide a better and complete whole picture.

Also, "friction" can be considered. What are some problems that one sees in the synchronic analysis? Identifying friction is a helpful methodological process in fine-tuning one's theories and conclusions. For instance, one can ask questions about the role of the Senate. Did they encourage the nucleus ritual? The electron rituals?

Now, it is important to point out that the methodological steps of identifying nucleus ritual, electron ritual, and the context of the atom are not necessarily linear in process. These are identified methodological necessities for a fruitful ritual studies. The final product will be organized with all these elements in mind in its own systematic way. It is likely that the nucleus ritual study will form the main thesis of the study, but this does not necessarily have to be the case, as a scientist could make the study of electrons, or an electron, in an atom as the main focus of the final report, although her study would have been a comprehensive one vis-a-vis that atom. An example of the application of my theory is provided below (without referral to the theoretical model of the atom) in the examination of Mithraism.

Mithraism – or the secret cult of Mithras – goes all the way back to Iran and Persian religions. According to Plutarch, conquered pirates transported to Italy by Pompey had a significant role in bringing it to Italy. M. J. Vermaseren attributes connection between pirates and intellectual segments of society as providing the channel for such transference of ideas. Taking Plutarch's account at face value, Pompey provides the terminus post quem for the spread of the cult of Mithraism. A problem exists in that no Mithraic monument can be dated earlier than the end of the first century AD. Even archaeologically plentiful Pompeii produced no remnant evidence of Mithraism under extensive search.[9] This has led certain scholars, such as Ulansey, to posit that

---

[9]M. J. Vermaseren, *Mithras, the Secret God* (London: Chatto & Windus, 1963) 28-29.

Mithraism spread throughout the Roman Empire in the first century AD.[10]

Whether the rise of Roman Mithraism is dated in the first century BC. or to the first century AD., one thing is clear – that is, it was a mystery religion with a cosmic significance. And astrology was an integral part of Mithraic cosmogony, as academic literature, such as Michael P. Seidel's *Mithras-Orion: Greek Hero and Roman Army God*, indicates.

Understanding the important relationship of astrology to Mithraism entails an examination of the socio-cultural context in which Mithraism rose. Hellenistic philosophy was an important aspect of the Graeco-Roman society. To be trained in rhetoric and philosophy was tantamount for success in the public, political, and private life. As A. A. Long and D. N. Sedley point out, Hellenistic philosophical schools took on characteristics somewhat different from preceding philosophical schools. This is evident in the comparison of Epicurus' perception of the soul (*psyche*) with previous philosophers. Aristotle understood the soul as embracing vital functions of any living thing – animals and plants. Plato's Phaedo presents the soul as an intellectual force housed in the animal body but separate from its functions and sensation. Long and Sedley note that Epicurus was "midway between these two extremes."[11] Epicurus explained: "The soul is a fine-structured body

---

[10] David Ulansey, *The Origins of the Mithraic Mysteries: Cosmology and Salvation in the Ancient World* (New York: Oxford University Press, 1989) 4.

[11] A. A. Long and D. N. Sedley, *The Hellenistic Philosophers (Vol. 1)* (Cambridge: Cambridge University Press, 1987) 70.

diffused through the whole aggregate, most strongly resembling wind with a certain blending of heat, and resembling wind in some respects but heat in others."[12] Long and Sedley note that Epicurus' emphasis on physicalist analysis reduced the soul to a mechanism.[13] Thus, two primary functions of the soul are consciousness in all aspects (sensations, thought, emotion) and transmission of the impulses of the body. In composition, the soul has two parts – the mind, in which thought and emotion are vocalized, and the spirit, which extends through the body and which works with the mind.[14]

Epicurus' emphasis on mechanistic process and physics is indicative of Hellenistic philosophical concern for explaining all things in terms of physics and scientific language. This is also evident in Epicurus' explanation of free will. Long and Sedley write: "It is perhaps the most widely known about Epicurus that he ... modified the deterministic Democritean system by introducing a slight element of indeterminacy to atomic motion, the 'swerve' ...."[15]

Hellenistic philosophy utilized such concepts as sense perception and atoms to describe human events and experiences, also. For instance, in describing friendship, Epicurus emphasizes its absolute necessity for happiness in line with popular Greek philosophy but adds comment on its mechanistic utility by claiming that friendship produces "kinetic"

---

[12]*Letter to Herodotus* 63-7.
[13]Long and Sedley 72.
[14]Long and Sedley 70-1.
[15]Long and Sedley 107.

pleasure[16] – meaning that friendship (and benefits in sense perception from friendship) outlast death.

Thus, for Hellenistic philosophy, there was cosmological significance to ordinary and human events and experiences. Stoicism provides a good example. Ulansey points out the active integration of astrology to Stoicism in this socio-cultural environment. Especially at the time of Zeno, Cleanthes, and Chrysippus, astrology became an integral part of the Stoic system and was championed as such with full cognizance. Astrology continued its influence in Stoicism, excepting for a short period of repudiation by Panaetius (c. 189-109 BC).[17] This reality in Stoicism is significant because Stoicism was the most important and influential Hellenistic philosophical school. W. W. Tarn notes: "The philosophy of the Hellenistic world was the Stoa; all else was secondary."[18]

There was an integral system for the harmonization of philosophical ideas as they played such a significant role in the public and private lives of the Romans. Roman mystery religion of Mithraism, encompassed significant developments in astrology. Mithraism, therefore, as a cosmic religion, promised for its initiates entrance to the cosmic reality. This is what Geertz calls, "world view," or peoples' sense of the "really real." By this, Geertz is

---

[16]Long and Sedley 145.
[17]Ulansey 71-72.
[18] W. W. Tarn, *Hellenistic Civilisation* (New York: New American Library, 1975) 325.

referring to the cognitive-existential aspects.[19] As Geertz describes world view, usually associated with beliefs, as being integrally connected to "ethos," or moral and aesthetic aspects of a culture, usually associated with religious ritual, Mithraism's cosmic reality has an accompanying central ritual – namely, tauroctony, or bull slaying.

In fact, it is this bull slaying that distinguishes Roman Mithraism from Iranian Mithraism. In the Iranian precedent, Mithras is not connected to bull slaying.[20] In regards to bull slaying of Mithras in Roman Mithraism, Ulansey posits an internal influence: "There has been a strong consensus among scholars of Mithraism that the origins of the artistic type of the Mithraic tauroctony can be traced back to earlier representations of Nike, the goddess victory, sacrificing a bull."[21]

The distinctiveness of tauroctony in Roman Mithraism is further underscored by the fact that depiction of tauroctony in iconographic[22] form is

---

[19]Catherine Bell, *Ritual Theory, Ritual Practice* (New York: Oxford University Press, 1992) 26.
[20]Ulansey 8-9.
[21]Ulansey 30.
[22]Diane Apostolos-Cappadona's concept of "mythic iconoclasm" and associated hermeneutical method for analyzing the situation of the "artist" and the "art work" is an interesting one and may provide some beneficial insights in the study of tauroctony and the ancient period ("Picasso's *Guernica* as Mythic Iconoclasm: An Eliadean Interpretation of the Myth of Modern Art" in Laurie L. Patton and Wendy Doniger (ed.), *Myth and Method* {Charlottesville and London: University Press of Virginia, 1996} 327). For Apostolos-Cappadona, "Iconoclasm is ... a creative activity" (331) and "*homo religiosus* is *homo aestheticus*" (347).

found in every mithraeum in its central place.[23] On the basis of this, Ulansey draws a conclusion regarding its centrality: "The fact that this iconographically fixed representation appeared in the most important place in every mithraeum forces us to conclude that it was of central importance to the cult's ideology and that its meaning, if we can decipher it, holds the key to the mystery of Mithraism."[24] For Ulansey, this meaning is a cosmological one. Ulansey writes: "Mithraic iconography was a cosmological code created by a circle of religious-minded philosophers and scientists to symbolize their possession of secret knowledge: namely, the knowledge of a newly discovered god so powerful that the entire cosmos was completely under his control."[25]

There have been other interpretations of the tauroctony. Some scholars have pointed out that the bull-slaying scene is actually emblematic of Mithras' victory over life and death. These scholars argue that in sacrificial enactments, the bull that is slayed represents Mithras and that he is seen as killed and

---

[23] There is practically no literary evidence, but since Mithraic temples (Mithraea) were often built underground, their contents were well-preserved. Thus, Mithraism is archaeologically very-well documented (Ulansey 3). Concerning archaeological evidence, Lucy Jayne Botscharow writes in agreement with Ricoeur: "An archaeological site is like a text in an unknown language. Like a written text, archaeology is fixed discourse.... Just as writing fixes the 'said' of speaking, so a given site fixes the 'said' of doing" ("Sites as Texts: An Exploration of Mousterian Traces" in Ian Hodder (ed.), *The Meaning of Things: Material Culture and Symbolic Expression* {London: Unwin Hyman, 1989} 50).
[24] Ulansey 6.
[25] Ulansey 125.

then resurrected.[26] Other scholars have seen tauroctony and sacrificial reenactment of it done in a cave[27] or a place appearing like a cave as a process by which the participants ritually relive the experience of the ritual.[28] Thus, each participant emerges triumphant.

Despite various interpretations that exist, they should not be perceived as mutually exclusive; in fact, the different interpretations can function in a complementary way to support Mithraism's cosmological claims.

In light of the cosmic significance of Mithraism at the time of the Roman Empire, each participant understood this ritual reenactment in cosmic sense. If so, it is not surprising why Mithraism held such a value for the Roman army to the extent that it became its official religion. What was particularly attractive for the followers of the cult of Mithras was the integral symbolization of victory. Vermaseren writes:

---

[26]Vermaseren 68-69.

[27]Although there were baptismal rites in Mithraism, the place of taurobolium in Mithraism is a controversial one. Taurobolium is particularly associated with the mystery religion of Cybele. There was, however, fraternal relationship between those belonging to the religion of Mithras, who were only men, and women of the religion of Cybele. There are inscriptions that refer to initiates of Mithraism with no connection with the religion with Cybele as *tauroboliati* (John Ferguson, *The Religions of the Roman Empire* {Ithaca: Cornell University Press, 1970} 112).

[28]Vermaseren 40.

> The god Mithras is always regarded as *deus invictus*, an invincible god, who as the Aresta records ... secures victory for his followers on the battlefield. In the struggle for the ultimate triumph of good over evil, Mithras is the associate of the god of good. Strictly speaking, every follower of the god was enrolled in his service (militia), but the special initiation and the taking of the military oath set the seal on entrance to his ranks.[29]

The examination of Mithraism shows the significance of the atomic study of a society and the forces that govern it – in terms of ritualization and ritual.

Of course, as it is my thesis and as it is in its incipient stages, more work needs to be done both on fine-tuning the theory and in the application of the atomic theory. Not without difficulties, this study clearly shows the merits of continuing on with the atomic approach. I am convinced that this approach – both applied to ritual theory – and in other types of studies employing sociology and anthropology will yield further advancement in knowledge and a greater breath of understanding.

---

[29]Vermaseren 144.

Bibliography

Bell, Catherine. *Ritual Theory, Ritual Practice*. New York: Oxford University Press, 1992.

Boissier, Gaston. *La Religion Romaine d'Auguste aux Antonins*. Paris: Librairie Hachette, 1874.

Burkert, Walter. *Structure and History in Greek Mythology and Ritual*. Berkeley: University of California Press, 1979.

Cassius Dio. *The Roman History: The Reign of Augustus*. Tr. Ian Scott-Kilvert. London: Penguin Books, 1987.

Ferguson, John. *The Religions of the Roman Empire*. Ithaca: Cornell University Press, 1970.

Gordon, R., S. Walker, and P. Zanker. *Image and Mystery in the Roman World*. Gloucester: Alan Sutton Publishing, 1988.

Hodder, Ian (Ed.). *The Meaning of Things: Material Culture and Symbolic Expression*. London: Unwin Hyman, 1989.

Jay, Nancy. *Throughout Your Generations Forever: Sacrifice, Religion, and Paternity*. Chicago and London: The University of Chicago Press, 1992.

Kirk, G. S. *The Nature of Greek Myths*. Harmondsworth: Penguin Books Ltd., 1974.

Liebeschuetz, J. H. W. G. *Continuity and Change in Roman Religion*. Oxford: Oxford University Press, 1979.

Long, A. A., and D. N. Sedley. *The Hellenistic Philosophers (Vol. 1)*. Cambridge: Cambridge University Press, 1987.

Patton, Laurie L., and Wendy Doniger (Ed.). *Myth and Method*. Charlottesville and London: University Press of Virginia, 1996.

Reinwald, Heinz. *Mythos und Methode: Zum Verhältnis von Wissenschaft, Kultur und Erkenntnis*. München: Wilhelm Fink Verlag, 1991.

Speidel, Michael P. *Mithras-Orion: Greek Hero and Roman Army God*. Leiden: E. J. Brill, 1980.

Syme, Ronald. *The Roman Revolution*. Oxford: Oxford University Press, 1939.

Tarn, W. W. *Hellenistic Civilisation*. New York: New American Library, 1975.

Ulansey, David. *The Origins of the Mithraic Mysteries: Cosmology and Salvation in the Ancient World*. New York: Oxford University Press, 1989.

Vermaseren, M. J. *Mithras, the Secret God*. London: Chatto & Windus, 1963.

Prophecy, Biblical Interpreters, and the Book of Chronicles[1]

Scholarship on post-exilic prophecy has been colored by monarchic concerns. Thus, presumption was that since classical prophecy was primarily tied to the court and since the Israelite court ceased to exist in the post-exilic prophecy, prophecy then must have ceased in the post-exilic period. Scholarship has, thus, been inclined to ignore prophecy in the post-exilic period, or to speak of prophecy in terms of decline.[2]

But a reconsideration of the question of the nature of prophecy in general and in the post-exilic period in particular will bring about a new understanding of prophecy in the post-exilic period. Even in the pre-exilic period, prophecy was not necessarily court bound. Various judges in the book of Judges, Moses, and Abraham provide examples of prophets who worked outside the context of the court from the textual narrative perspective. Furthermore, even during the monarchic period, there were prophets, such as Amos and Hosea, who worked

---

[1] This paper was written in the context of the Ph.D. program in Judaic Studies at Brown University in 1998.

[2] William M. Schiedewind writes: "Discussion of post-exilic prophecy has often focused on the 'decline', 'demise', or 'end' of prophecy. A decline of prophecy depends on a particular definition of prophecy" ("Prophets and Prophecy in the Book of Chronicles," The Chronicler as Historian, ed. M. Patrick Graham, Kenneth G. Hoglund, and Steven L. McKenzie [Sheffield: Sheffield Academic Press, 1997, pp. 204-224] 206).

outside the immediate court context. Thus, understanding of prophets as necessarily court-bound is faulty. And on top of this consideration of the general question of prophecy in ancient Israel lies the particular question of prophecy in the post-exilic period. In the post-exilic period, there are descriptions of prophets in the classical sense. That is to say, there are attestations in the post-exilic composition, such as the books of Chronicles that, at least in part, reflect the concerns and interests of the Sitz im Leben of the composer(s), which describe prophets in the classical sense – namely, that of court prophets. On the other hand, there are other class of prophets that gain prominence in the post-exilic period, who would not fit into the definition of prophets in the classical sense. These are biblical interpreters, who gain ascendancy as the part of the developing Temple culture.

In this paper, I will consider at a greater detail the questions relating to the nature of prophecy in general and of its nature in the post-exilic period in particular, especially as described by the Chronicler. Since the focus of the study is related to prophecy in the post-exilic period, I will study the "classical prophets" in contrast to the "biblical interpreters." Of course, the discussion will involve definition as well as explication.

Furthermore, this study will benefit from examination of the Chronicler. I argue that the Chronicler also belonged to the new class of prophets, namely the "biblical interpreters." This is innately clear in his utilization of his sources.[3] He reinterprets the Jerusalem Temple in terms of its supremacy by privileging it over and against the monarchy. Thus, David and Solomon, who receive much attention in the books of Chronicles, obtain their value because they were involved in the building of the Temple.

Even the literary device of prayers (of David and Solomon) props up the authority of the Temple. The authority of the Temple is further affirmed as the text relating to its building utilizes imagery that hearken back to the Tabernacle. In fact, since the Temple receives such a privileging over against the monarchy, king's value is estimated in that regard. Thus, the northern Israelite kings are all but ignored. And Saul is seen as a bad king because he had no interest in the cult; not only did he not participate in the building or planning for the Temple, he also did not bring the ark to Jerusalem.

The supremacy of the Jerusalem Temple is important since that is essential to prop up the authority of the biblical interpreters, whose authority is innately tied to the Temple cultus. Furthermore, since the monarchy no longer existed, history had to be reinterpreted[4] to focus on the Temple as the

---

[3] Some scholars posit that the Chronicler freely offered his interpretation because his audience was merely familiar with the history represented in his sources and were not interested in conducting any detailed synoptic study. One such scholar is Rodney K. Duke, who argues that this condition allowed Chronicler to submit his work as a rhetorical writing of persuasion (The Persuasive Appeal of the Chronicler: A Rhetorical Analysis [Sheffield: Almond Press, 1990] 37).

[4] Peter R. Ackroyd, therefore, argues: "For the real point is to see the Chronicler not as a poor historian or as a good historian,

primarily *telos* of history which Yahweh was leading. In this, the Chronicler was not only reflecting the concerns of his community, but providing the intellectual underpinnings for why and how the things are the way they are and that there is no reason for despair on the part of his community.

In order to properly understand prophecy in the post-exilic period, some consideration of prophecy in general terms need to be considered. Understanding of classical prophecy as necessarily tied to ancient Israelite monarchy needs to be reassessed based on various attestations in the Hebrew Bible that reflect a contrasting reality.

The judges in the book of Judges provide a type of prophets who are not bound to the court. The setting of the book necessarily precludes a monarchy-centric prophecy and prophets. In fact, the Judges themselves function as a type of pre-monarchs. They lead the Israelites into military victory. When one examines the function of kings in the Deuteronomistic history, this was one of the primary function of ancient Israelite and Judaean kings.

These judges, however, do not bring message of repentance to the Israelite people, rather they function as tools of deliverance. Yet, it would not be altogether accurate to say that they do not function in the process of repentance of the ancient Israelites.

---

but as an interpreter. He handles the older traditions; he incorporates newer material in them; he rearranges, comments, elaborates, sermonizes – all with the purposes of bringing home to his reader (or perhaps his hearers, for the style is very strongly homiletic), the meaning for themselves of what is being related and expounded" (The Chronicler in His Age [Sheffield: Sheffield Academic Press, 1991] 276).

They, in fact, often mirror the ancient Israelites in their regression as was the case with Samson. Although from the textual perspective, it is not clear, as in the case of Hosea, that Samson's behavior was a form of prophetic-symbolic re-enactment, these judge-prophets functioned as a leading voice of the ancient Israelites.

The leadership role that judges played in the deliverance of Israelites is not altogether different from that of the prophets during the monarchic period. Prophets in the monarchic period participated in the deliverance of the Israelite people. It is true that they often functioned in this regard in their assistance of kings. Kings sought their oracles, hoping for victory. However, in the textual representation that both judges and monarchic prophets represented cultic agents of deliverance, they share similar function and role. So it would not be too far-fetched to view judges as "prophets".

Besides the judges, there are others in the Hebrew Bible who are prophets outside the context of ancient Israelite court. One such example is Moses. In fact, when one examines the prophetic call of Moses in Exodus 3-4, one finds that it serves as a model for other prophetic calls, such as the call of Isaiah in Isaiah 6 and the call of Jeremiah in Jeremiah 1. The most marked feature of the call of Moses is his protest. One sees that Moses protests five times during his call (Ex. 3.11; 3:13; 4:1; 4:10; 4:13) and each time the text presents Yahweh's response to the protest. This protest element serves to genrify (or to provide a genre of literature) the nature of prophetic call narratives. Accordingly one sees in Jeremiah 1:6 that Jeremiah protests to the prophetic call.

As it is in the Exodus account in relation to Moses, Jeremiah's protest is met with Yahweh's response. Thus, in both the prophetic call of Moses and Jeremiah, problem raised by prophets are met by resolution/solution by Yahweh. It is further worthy of note that the protest by Moses and by Jeremiah share the same protest – namely, that they are not good with words. In both cases, the solution by Yahweh directly involves meeting this need.

In the prophetic call of Isaiah, it appears that possibly the call of Moses does not serve as a model of Isaiah's prophetic call. In Isaiah 6:8, Isaiah readily accepts the call to be Yahweh's prophet. However, one sees that Isaiah does offer a form of protest in Isaiah 6:5. Granted, the protest is not directly aimed at the prophetic call per se; however, it does concern his own holiness. This is significant in light of the fact that Yahweh's holy attributes are emphasized in verse three. How could an unholy person represent holy Yahweh? This problem is resolved in Isaiah's sanctification in Isaiah 6:6-7. One could argue that it is this resolution that allows for Isaiah's ready acceptance of the prophetic call. Thus, the call of Isaiah could be seen as a slight modification of the call narrative formula represented in Exodus 3 and 4.

How is it significant that the prophetic call of Moses serves as a model of the prophetic calls of such figures as Isaiah and Jeremiah? The prophetic call of Moses is very important in understanding the nature of prophecy and prophets in the monarchic period. The very fact that the prophetic calls of prophets in monarchic period were modeled after the prophetic call of Moses points to the fact that prophets did not derive their primary characteristics in reference to the monarchy. The composer(s) of Exodus 3 and 4, by placing Moses' call in a prophetic call genre, was implicitly recognizing the possibility of a "real" prophet, whose existence was not dependent on the monarchy. Thus, understanding prophets as necessarily tied to the court would be a misleading assumption.

What would, then, be a positive assertion regarding the nature and function of prophets that one can make from the reality that Moses served as a prophet, and possibly an arch-type of a prophet at that? Prophets in ancient Israel were concerned with religion and worship of Yahweh. The fact that Israelite and Judaean prophets were tied to monarchy does not define them; it was merely the result of circumstances. Thus, it necessarily follows that their legitimacy is tied to Israelite religion and to no other factors. Just as prophets existed before the monarchy (definitely on the narrative level), they continued to exist after the cessation of Israelite monarchy and kingdoms. Thus, the example of Moses is a significant one in understanding Israelite prophecy.

Besides Moses, there are also other prophets, whose setting is found in the pre-monarchic period. One such figure is Abraham. He is referred to as a prophet in Genesis 20:7. On a narrative level, it is significant that this claim is placed in the lips of the ancient Israelite God. Within the internal dynamics of the text, Abraham's duties include appeasement of divine wrath on Abimelech by his prayer. This representation of Abraham as prophet is consistent with the portrayal of prophets as representatives of Israelite religion and shares with the picture of prophets found in the book of Judges. This representation of Abraham as a prophet is consistent with the nature of prophets as being tied to religion and not necessarily to monarchy.

Abraham's function as a prophet is also further represented in other texts. When one examines the binding of Isaac passage in Genesis 22, one sees that Abraham is called to go to the land of Moriah and sacrifice in one of the mountains that Yahweh will show him (verse two). This is reminiscent of the Yahweh's directive to Moses found in Exodus 3:12. In a similar way, Moses is commanded to go and sacrifice in the place that Yahweh will show him.

It is, therefore, no surprise that Medieval Torah commentators, such as Ibn Ezra, have noted that the place that Yahweh was to show Abraham is the same place where the Israelites were to sacrifice their offerings and build their Temple. Rashi even comments that the term Moriah is derived from the fact that the place was where the sacrifice of incense Myrrh was to occur. Ramban goes as far as to state that the place is where Cain and Abel, Noah and his sons offered their first sacrifice. What these medieval Torah commentators underscore is the crucial role of Abraham and Moses to Israelite religion and worship of Yahweh.

Thus, Abraham and Moses are prophets who do not need kings to give them legitimacy. This, in turn, points to the reality that classical prophecy and prophets were not bound to Israelite monarchy. But it would be wrong to argue that Abraham and Moses were not bound to the court merely on account of their narrative setting, and not as a matter of principle. For, if one examines certain prophets who worked during the period of the monarchy, one sees that they do not neatly fit into the image of prophets tied to the monarchy. Two examples will suffice.

Amos is actually a dresser of Sycamore trees and a sheep herder,[5] but he was called to be a prophet. His prophetic service was not bound to court settings. In fact, he worked as an itinerant and independent prophet. His message was addressed to the nobility of Israel and concerned issues relating to social justice. Scholars have commented on the absence of the direct concern for monarchy and monarchic interests, and a concern more on an individual level.[6] But one may note that scholarly attention to lack of monarchic interest in the book of Amos is motivated by a model of perception of prophecy that sees its essential characteristic as court-bound. What is to say that Amos' prophetic activity is out of the "norm"? The picture of court prophets are primarily presented by the Deuteronomistic Historian and may represent only that perspective. The primary interest of the Deuteronomistic Historian geared toward Royal Ideology and Zion Theology. In fact, they were two sides of the same coin and operated together. It was in the interest of the Deuteronomistic Historian to prop up royal authority. In light of this intent of the

---

[5]Amos 1:1; 7:14
[6]On the individualism emphasis, see the discussion in Shalom M. Paul, Amos (Minneapolis: Fortress Press, 1991).

Deuteronomistic Historian, it is not difficult to see why it would be in their interest to portray the powerful institution of prophecy and prophets as essentially tied to kings and as deriving their legitimacy innately through their relation to and interaction with monarchs and monarchy.

Besides Amos, Hosea provides a picture of prophecy in ancient Israel even during the monarchy period, which would be different from the monarchy-centric position. Hosea was a prophet, who was born a priest. Hosea had kept himself ritually pure all his life. Yet, Yahweh tells him to marry a prostitute, named Gomer, which would be tantamount to defiling himself according to the regulations for priestly marriage. To make matters worse in this regard, Gomer was a participant in Baal Harvest Festival orgies. More than once, Hosea had to go and reclaim his wife, from these celebrations. By his actions, Hosea was representing in symbolic action the way Israelites have acted before Yahweh – acting as violators of their covenental relationship. This prophetic activity of Amos, certainly was addressed to people at large and not necessarily to the Israelite monarchy. Thus, Hosea provides another picture of prophecy and prophets in the monarchic period, which does not have integral ties with the monarchy for its characteristic nature and function.[7]

How is all this consideration of prophecy and prophets in the "pre-Chronicles period" relevant for understanding prophecy and prophets in the books of the Chronicles? For one, when one understands that

---

[7]Helpful is discussion on Hosea by Hans Walter Wolff, Hosea (Philadelphia: Fortress Press, 1974).

prophecy was never innately bound to monarchy and that prophets never derived their essential identity from it, one understands that the portrayal of prophets in the book of Chronicles do not necessarily deviate from the previous portrayals.

One can divide the prophets in the books of Chronicles into two categories: prophets who primarily addressed kings and prophets who were essentially biblical interpreters who addressed the people. Although this categorization may, on the surface, seem to provide a differing view of prophecy in the post-exilic period, a closer examination betrays this surface review. Indeed, as was noted, one finds prophets who addressed the king as well as those who addressed the people. Of course, these two groups of audience are not mutually exclusive in terms of the prophetic activity of prophets.

Then, how did we come up with the two categories? The ideas of William Schniedewind is helpful in assessing the two categories. Schniedewind divides two categories based on the use of specific terms used to describe the prophets. Thus, prophets who are described in terms traditionally/classically referring to the prophets, such as "prophet", "seer", "seer", and "man of God" belong to one class of prophets,[8] and prophets who do not have these designation, but who are "inspired messengers,"[9] belong to the other class. Although this is an arbitrary division, it turns out that those who are associated with classical terms for prophets are described in the books of Chronicles as primarily

---

[8] Schniedewind (1997) 214.
[9] Schniedewind (1997) 222.

addressing the kings, whereas inspired messengers address the people.[10]

The other category of prophets, the inspired messengers, form a category almost by default. These are prophets who are not described in terms classically associated with prophets. However, they have certain attributes that are congruent with functions of the prophets in the "pre-Chronicles period." For one, those who belong to the second category are also presented as representatives of Yahweh on the religious level. Furthermore, they are described as speaking the words of Yahweh. Schniedewind aptly points out a major difference: "The messenger of YHWH requires an inspiration formula, whereas the prophet may speak in YHWH's behalf without a[n] inspiration formula."[11]

An inspiration formula that is often applied to inspired messengers are "the spirit clothed..." and "the spirit came upon..." Schniedewind refers to these two formulae as "possession formulas" and states: "The possession formulas are used with priests, Levites and soldiers as an indication of divine authority, but not with prophets [in the classical sense]."[12] In contrast, traditional prophetic formulae, such as "Thus says YHWH" and "the word of YHWH came to," are used with those who have classical prophetic titles.[13]

---

[10]Schniedewind (1997) 219.
[11]William M. Schniedewind, The Word of God in Transition: From Prophets to Exegete in the Second Temple Period (Sheffield: Sheffield Academic Press, 1995) 85.
[12]Schniedewind (1995) 70.
[13]Schniedewind (1995) 78-79.

This has led some scholars to note that these biblical interpreters provide a picture into the reality of the Chronicler's Sitz im Leben. Chronicler's setting was one in which the institution of monarchy no longer existed. The Second Temple had been rebuilt and religious authority was maintained primarily by those who were associated with the Temple. There was a need to explain why the current situation was the way it was. Why did Yahweh allow the institution of the monarchy not to be restored? Was not the house of David forever? Was the royal ideology that had been so dominant throughout the years been wrong? If indeed Yahweh delivered the exiles and returned in full glory to Zion, in keeping with Zion theology, did it not necessarily follow that royal ideology, the flip-side of the same coin, should be restored, too?

But the current situation of the time did not see the restoration of a Davidide to the throne. So, how was this to be explained? Was not Yahweh all powerful? Did Yahweh make a mistake? For the Chronicler, the answer could not be a "yes." Since Yahweh was all powerful in the thought of the Chronicler, he was compelled to re-explain history in terms that would make Yahweh look good and portray the situation of his time as a normative one. How did he go about doing this?

The primary means by which the Chronicler achieved his goals was to privilege the institution of the Temple over and against all other ideologies and institutions, such as the royal ideology and the institution of the monarchy. In fact, the Chronicler re-explained history, so that all the past events were contributing to the elevation of the Temple and its service. Not only that, he further gave value to the Temple, by elevating the function and character of those who were at his time involved in its service and teaching.

In fact, he describes the biblical interpreters of his time, which included (and perhaps because it included) him, [14] to the status of the prophets. Prophets actually formed the most continuous institution in ancient Israelite history, since it is described in literature as having existed since the patriarchal times. Showing continuity in this religious institution, therefore, was quite important. It was in this continuity that Yahweh's faithfulness to his people was exhibited.

Let us first consider what was the primary means by which the Chronicler privileged the Temple and its service over and against all other ideologies and institutions. First of all, in the Chronicler's historiography, there is an elevation of the status of Judaea and its kingdom, which was the seat of the Jerusalem Temple. The kings of the northern Israelite kingdom, therefore, are not represented well

---

[14]Schniedewind writes: "It is quite possible that Chr saw himself in a role similar to his inspired messengers. Chr speaks primarily to the people, that is, to the post-exilic community. The various aspects of Chr's composition – speeches, narrative style, and theology – all serve a homiletic function. And in particular, the prophetic narratives in chronicles cannot be understood simply by the context of their First Temple referents; they are primarily directed toward the post-exilic community" ([1997] 222).

in terms of quantity and also of quality in the narratives of the Chronicler.[15]

On the contrary, David is emphasized. He is seen as the legitimate founder of the Judean kingdom. In this sense, one could argue that the remnant of the royal ideology could be found. However, even if one were to argue that royal ideology did leave a lasting imprint in Israelite history and its historiography, it would be hard to argue that the attention paid to David in the books of Chronicles was due to the Chronicler's allegiance to the royal ideology. It would be more accurate to view Chronicler's portrayal in terms of his privileging the Temple and Israelite religion. William Riley writes:

> When the Chronicler's political situation (the continuing absence of a Davidic regent) and liturgical situation (the continued celebration of the Davidic covenant) are taken together, the Chronicler's portrayal of David and his house in cultic terms may be seen as an emphasis on the religious contribution that the dynasty has made and as a disavowal of the necessity for a post-exilic Davidic successor to the throne of Israel.[16]

---

[15] Martin Noth, The Chronicler's History, trans. H. G. M. Williamson (Sheffield: Sheffield Academic Press, 1987) 89-91.
[16] King and Cultus in Chronicles: Worship and the Reinterpretation of History (Sheffield: Sheffield Academic Press, 1993) 35.

David and royal ideology based on his rule derived intrinsic value from the Temple and Israelite religion in the writing of the Chronicler.

Emphasis on the Temple is the Chronicler's over-arching theme. This becomes more lucid in light of the question: Was not Saul the founder of the Judaean kingdom? This is a valid question and has truth to it, since the Deuteronomistic Historian does give a fair amount of attention to Saul. However, for the Chronicler, Saul does not have real value. Since value referent for the Chronicler is the Temple and since Saul has no value in his sources (chief being that of the Deuteronomistic Historian) in this regard, Saul is only given a cursory attention. Furthermore, it should be remembered that David is attributed with having brought the ark of the covenant to Jerusalem,[17] whereas Saul is described as having let the ark of the covenant stay in oblivion. The Chronicler exhibits resentment toward Saul for this action.

It is precisely because David had an important role to play in the Israelite religion that the Chronicler attributes value to him by dedicating a significant portion to him. Royal ideology is only

---

[17]Duke writes: "There is a reciprocal bond between David's actions in 'establishing' the official cultic forms for worshipping Yahweh (1 Chron. 15.1, 3, 12; 22.3, 5, 14; 28.2; 29.2, 3, 19; 2 Chron. 1.4; 2.6) and Yahweh's promises and actions in regard to 'establishing' the Davidic kingdom (1 Chron. 14.2; 17.11, 12, 14, 24; 22.10; 28.7). For example, the above declaration (14.2) accompanied by illustrations of David's successful rule in the rest of the chapter came after his attempt to bring the ark to Jerusalem (ch. 13). The scene found in the following chapters (15-16) again portrays David establishing the cult of Yahweh" (58-59).

secondary to the Chronicler's Temple-phile position. Thus, the Chronicler describes David as spending much time and energy preparing for the Temple. In this way, David is not merely the rejected Temple builder of the Deuteronomistic Historian's account, but rather he is an integral first step to the building of the Jerusalem Temple. And Solomon provides the important second and completing step to the Temple building project. Peter R. Ackroyd thus writes: "In the book of Chronicles ... David is the founder and organizer of temple worship, including the priestly and other personnel; Solomon carries through the building of the temple which David has prepared and committed to him."[18]

David and Solomon's value as essentially tied to the Jerusalem Temple project is further highlighted in light of the literary device of the prayer found in the books of Chronicles. There are various prayers of David (1 Chr. 14:10; 16:8-36; 17:16-27; 21:8, 17; 29:10-19) and those of Solomon (2 Chr. 1:8-10; 5:13; 7:3, 6; 6:14-42) found in the books of Chronicles which parallel each other and forms an inverted chiastic structure within the narrative reality pointing toward and "sandwiching" the Temple building account (2 Chr. 2:1-5:1) in the books of Chronicles.[19] The fact that a complex literary structure points toward the Temple in Jerusalem definitively accent-

---

[18] 225.
[19] Samuel E. Balentine, "'You Can't Pray a Lie': Truth and Fiction in the Prayers of Chronicles," The Chronicler as Historian, ed. M. Patrick Graham, Kenneth G. Hoglund and Steven L. McKenzie (Sheffield: Sheffield Academic Press, 1997, pp. 246-267) 258-267.

tuates the overriding concern of the Chronicler to privilege the Temple in his historiography.

The privileging of the Temple is clear from the fact that the Chronicler devotes so much of his book to the Temple building account in the books of the Chronicles. The striking feature of this description is that the Chronicler uses the same language in describing the Temple building account in the books of Chronicles as the Temple building account found in the Deuteronomistic historian. One would expect that the experience of the building of the Second Temple would significantly shift the Temple description to be more in align with the Second Temple, but the fact that the Chronicler is faithful (at least from the literary perspective) in the description of the Temple to his sources, namely the Deuteronomistic Historian, shows the Chronicler's lasting concern with maintaining the ideal of the Jerusalem Temple.

In fact, this ideal of the Jerusalem Temple plays such a significant role in the historical consciousness of the Chronicler that where his account of the Jerusalem Temple varies with the account offered by the Deuteronomistic Historian, there is even a hearkening further back to the description of the Tabernacle. John Van Seters argues:

> The nature of Chr's historiography is deliberately and consciously ideological. Only one of his sources – the book of Kings – purports to describe the Solomonic temple. The information from this source he deliberately modifies to bring it into closer agree-

ment with that of the tabernacle to create a more obvious continuity with the law of Moses in its Priestly form than would otherwise be the case.[20]

This is in tune with the concern with the Chronicler to portray the current state of affairs in his environment as a continuous process of history guided by Yahweh. Just as the Second Temple is a continuation of the First Temple, both of them provide a continuation of the Tabernacle, the arch-type of the Temple. This further highlights the religion-centric concern of the Chronicler. The chief constant in Israelite history for the Chronicler is the continuous religious history centered on the worship of Yahweh.

Indeed, the Jerusalem Temple represented a historical constant for the Chronicler, and, therefore, the Chronicler was interested in reinterpreting his history in terms of this position. In other words, the Chronicler's historiography privileged the Temple and its service above all else. Thus, it is not surprising that even the prophets gain ascendancy and are linked more with the Temple and its service.

The reminiscence to the tabernacle in the Chronicler's description of the Temple is a case in point. Moses, the arch-typical prophet, was operative outside of the monarchic system. His primarily loyalty was to Yahweh and in his worship. The Tabernacle as a pre-temple, represented a precedent

---

[20]"The Chronicler's Account of Solomon's Temple-Building: A Continuity Theme," The Chronicler as Historian, ed. M. Patrick Graham, Kenneth G. Hoglund and Steven L. McKenzie (Sheffield: Sheffield Academic Press, 1997, pp. 283-300) 300.

for the supremacy of the Temple and participants in its worship, to which group, the Chronicler appended the prophets. Thus, although the classical monarchic prophets who are described in terms of *nabi*, *roeh*, *hozeh*, and *ish-elohim*, while portrayed as addressing the king, their primary reference point and allegiance is to Yahweh and his worship, and particularly that which is tied to the Jerusalem Temple.

Thus, the other "class" of prophets, the biblical interpreters, who were mainly operative in the contemporary social framework of the Chronicler, gain ascendancy in position by the virtue of the fact that they belong to the class of prophets and are directly linked to the ecstatic prophets of the previous generations. The Chronicler's interest in this portrayal of the biblical interpreters is quite obvious – he perceived himself to be a part of this new "class" of prophets.

In fact, in the description of the classical prophets in the books of Chronicles, although they may be described as primarily addressing the Kings, they are seen as representatives of the Temple and Yahweh's service. Especially in light of the fact that the Chronicler portrays the king's existence and legitimacy particularly in relation to their support of the Temple, the role of classical prophets are reinterpreted. They are not servants of the court per se, but rather primarily in service of the Temple and Yahweh.

Furthermore, biblical interpreters provide another class of prophets whose heritage is closely tied to this reinterpreted version of classical prophets. These biblical interpreters are more directly tied to the Temple and its service. This can be seen as an intentional strategic description. The socio-historical reality of the Chronicler was that the Temple in Jerusalem existed, but the monarchy did not. The Chronicler had to explain who these new class of biblical interpreters were. The Chronicler did not want to outright claim that they are prophets, since there was a received tradition of who the prophets were. We need to understand that the Chronicler's source was readily available. After all, the Chronicler had access to them, so why not others?

This in connection with the collective memory of the "classical" prophets limited the Chronicler in his attempt to claim outright that the new class of biblical interpreters, among whose group the Chronicler included himself, were prophets in the classical sense. Thus, the Chronicler strategically attributes to them qualities that normally pertain to prophets. Thus, the key expressions as those found in the possession (of the spirit) formulae came to them are reminiscent of the prophetic call of classical prophets. It is further significant that the function of these biblical interpreters share significantly with the function of classical prophets. Chief among them is the fact that the biblical interpreters represent, or purport to represent, Yahweh and his interests.

Because of the predominant trend in scholarship toward understanding the prophets and prophecy as essentially tied to the monarchy, scholars have often described the situation of prophecy in the post-exilic period in terms of decline. The exilic period may provide the chief explanatory factor. It may be possible to argue that prophets of the pre-exilic period were no longer needed because they succeeded. Indeed, there seemed to be prophets in the pre-exilic period whose primary activity seemed to be to show how the Israelites would be carried away into the exile. A good example is Jeremiah's carrying a beam on his shoulders to show that the Israelites would be carried away into the exile. Once this prophecy is fulfilled, this kind of prophetic activity no longer becomes necessary.

It is also possible to explain "the decline of prophecy" in terms of failure of pre-exilic prophets. The fact that Israelites were carried into exile represented the failure of the prophets to turn the Israelites toward faithfulness to Yahweh and his worship. It is their failure compounded with the experience of the exile that propelled the decline of the institution of prophecy and of prophets.

In light of our study that the Chronicler portrayed the biblical interpreters as a kind of prophets, the whole dialogue of the "decline" of prophecy and prophets in ancient Israel becomes a mute discussion. Prophecy and prophets did not decline or cease. Rather, biblical interpreters represented continuation of the prophecy and prophets that had been more tied with monarchy when it existed.

In the absence of monarchy, there was no possibility that any prophecy would be tied to monarchy. This kind of prophetic tradition not tied to monarchy existed also in the period of the monarchy as was shown, as well as period in the pre-monarchic period. Thus, there is no viable reason to assert that prophecy declined or ceased in the post-exilic period. It was in the post-exilic period that biblical interpreters represented Yahweh and his religious interests and propagated his message in a form that was more distinctive to their socio-historical setting. Thus, it is no surprise that elevation of biblical interpretation is seen in the redefinition of the "word of God." For Schniedewind, Chronicler's time represented a period in which the word of Yahweh referred not only to the prophetic oracle but also to written texts sacred to him and his community. Schniedewind writes:

> Chronicles resignifies the very term which classical prophecy uses for the prophetic word, that is the "word of YHWH" (דבר יהוה). No longer is the "word of YHWH" simply the prophetic oracle; Chronicles now also uses the "word of YHWH" to refer to "the law of Moses" (תורת משה). [21] Chronicles not only expands the meaning of the term for the prophetic word, it also revises the words of prophecy themselves. The Chronicler actually alters and recontextualizes prophecies from Samuel-Kings. By reinterpreting the word of God, the Chronicler gives it new meaning in the context of his rewritten history of

---

[21] Thus, Duke writes: "With the Chronicler one finds a trait characteristic of the post-exilic community. The Torah was regarded as authoritative. It had become or was becoming regarded as sacred Scripture" (114).

Israel. This reinterpretation and re-contextualization of the word of God undoubtedly reflects the transition which took place in the sixth century BCE, a transition from a kingdom to a people.[22]

In assessing the function and role of prophecy in the books of Chronicles, Sitz im Leben of the Chronicler is thus very important. The Chronicler's socio-historical environment propelled him to privilege the Temple in his re-writing of Israel's history. In that sense, the Chronicler was interested in portraying a particular reality that reflected his situation and he worked to legitimate the existent socio-religious structure of his time – to which he belonged. He was a part of the biblical interpreter "guild" and he was interested in deriving legitimacy from ancient precedents.

In this light, the question of audience is not too difficult to answer. The audience is the Israelite community of the post-exilic period who were present in Judaea. It was in the Chronicler's interest to prop up the authority of the biblical interpreters. Also, the Chronicler was interested in providing an explanation for the post-exilic community for why the monarchy no longer existed. If in fact, the chief purpose of the monarchy was to buttress the Temple and Yahweh's worship, then the disappearance of that institution is not such a terrible thing, especially since the Jerusalem Temple physically stood before the community of the Second Temple period.

---

[22]Schniedewind (1995) 130.

One should give due attention to the argument forwarded by Von Rad and others that the book of Chronicles might have had as one of its audience, the Samaritans – or, rather, that its intent was to function as a apologetic literature for the Jerusalem Temple. Martin Noth writes: "Chr.'s central concern was to demonstrate the legitimacy of the Davidic dynasty and of the Jerusalem temple as Yahweh's valid cult centre. .... The opposition whom Chr. had in view can only have been the Samaritan community with a cult of their own on Mt Gerizim."[23] In this light, the Chronicler could be seen as taking the logical step from those of the Deuteronomistic Historian.

Particularly, in light of the hind sight of the exile, the Chronicler was interested in strengthening the Jerusalem Temple center and privileging Yahweh's worship at that site. This would provide an explanation for why the Chronicler decreases the treatment of the northern kingdom of Israel in his narrative description of the history of ancient Israel. The difference is somewhat marked when one places the Chronicler's account next to that of the Deuteronomistic Historian. It is also possible that the Chronicler perceived that it was the mistake of the Deuteronomistic Historian to give certain attention to the northern kingdom in his treatment. Perhaps, the Chronicler blames the exile on the "sins" of the northern kingdom, which had cultic sites that existed apart from the Jerusalem Temple. The Chronicler was interested in seeing worship of Yahweh only in Jerusalem and the centralization of the religion there. This could be due to his theological understanding

---

[23] 100.

(which actually was most likely in tune in large part with the Deuteronomistic Historian) as well as socio-political concerns. When one considers the radical injunction against intermarriage in Ezra-Nehemiah and also a primary concern for Sabbath day observance, one comes to the position that at least one faction – perhaps the ruling faction – had a strict and radical reinterpretation of the earlier sources to bring about religious centralization and prop up religious authority focused on the Jerusalem Temple so that another exile would not occur as the result of Yahweh's displeasure. It was a socio-political action motivated by past experience of the exile filtered through the lenses of the Deuteronomistic Historian.

It is important to note that the biblical interpreter tradition found and privileged in the book of Chronicles is not unique to the book of Chronicles and to the Chronicler. Biblical interpretation functioning in an authoritative way continued to gain ascendancy in later texts and provide a possible diachronic reality.

Indeed, at the center was the Jerusalem Temple. The Jerusalem Temple was so important in the post-exilic self-consciousness that it pervaded the liturgy of the Second Temple period and even after the destruction of the Second Temple in 70 AD continued to play an important role in religious consciousness and liturgical reality. It is not surprising that prophecy and prophets in the post-exilic period came to be tied integrally with the Jerusalem-focused religion.

Food, Eating Practices, and Empowerment in the Narratives of Acts[1]

In Acts, food and eating practices portray forms of empowerment (which means in this paper: giving socialized authority and legitimacy to participate in the in-group social activities) and dynamics of power politics. Breaking of bread, often accompanied by didactic conversation, empowered the breaker of bread and participants. Some narratives in Acts, especially related to instances of eating practices, address the question of the legitimacy of gentile participation in these eating practices, or breaking of bread, and concurrent empowerment. Narratives surrounding kerygmae of Peter represent efforts to shift primary reference points, such as circumcision, for defining who can or cannot participate in eating practices. Although narratives in Acts portray Peter successfully expanding the framework for social referencing and for participation in eating practices, they also present the concern of James and the Jerusalem leadership interested in moderating gentile empowerment through food regulation. In this draft, I will study texts in Acts that are relevant to food and eating practices and the question of gentile empowerment associated with them. And then, I will examine the possibility that the symposion and open table fellowship of Jesus of

---

[1] I would like to thank Professor Stanley Stowers of Brown University for reading the complete paper and commenting on it. This paper was written in 1998.

Nazareth had of being historical precedents to breaking of bread narratives in the book of Acts. Furthermore, I will consider the symbol and function of the Temple as a literary contrast to the household (and the breaking of bread, usually done in the household) and consider John Elliott's views on the issue.

In the book of Acts, eating is a form of empowerment. Eating fellowship is a way to suggest authority. Those who eat with a person who has authority (or is perceived as having authority) necessarily provides a social authority to the participants. This case is visible in the kerygma attributed to Peter in Acts 10:34-43, in which he points to his authority by referring to his being among the "chosen", those who ate and drank with Jesus in his last days. The narrative attributes to the mouth of Peter: "He [Jesus] was not seen by all the people, but by witnesses whom God had already chosen – by us who ate and drank with him after he rose from the dead" (Acts 10:41 NIV). The participation in eating practices with Jesus forms the conceptual endowment of social authority in the kerygma attributed to Peter in Acts 10:34-43.

Acts 1:4-5 provides another evidence that those who participates in eating with a person with social authority gain a part of that authority: "On one occasion, while he [Jesus] was eating with them, he gave them this command: 'Do not leave Jerusalem, but wait for the gift my Father promised, which you have heard me speak about. For John baptized with water, but in a few days you will be baptized with the Holy Spirit'" (NIV). It was in the context of the eating practice that the participants are promised a form of social authority, described in terms of baptism by the Holy Spirit.

But Acts 1:4-5 does more than provide a picture of how participants get a form of social authority, the passage further shows that the authoritative individual gives a didactic message in conjunction with eating practices.

The fact that eating practices were often coupled with a didactic message by the breaker of bread is clear in Acts 20. In fact, one sees that "breaking of bread" functions here as a seemingly necessary component to didactic conversation. Acts 20:7 describes: "On the first day of the week we came together to break bread. Paul spoke to the people and, because he intended to leave the next day, kept on talking until midnight" (NIV). It is important to notice that breaking of bread is recognized on the literary level, even if not in an actual level,[2] as a ritualized practice that gathered the people, and in this context Paul seized the opportunity to speak before his departure. The breaking of bread provided Paul with social authority and the environment in which Paul could speak.

---

[2] By "actual level" I refer to the possibility that the narrative describes the breaking of bread being done twice, in verse seven and verse eleven. However, for the purposes of my argument, the actual breaking of bread is not so important. What is important is that on the literary level, the author/redactor includes the term of "breaking of bread" before didactic speech. I would posit that this is strategic and points to the understanding that breaking of bread socially ordered the breaker of the bread to an authoritative position, in which his words are heeded by the participants.

In the narrative, the conversation does not end at midnight; it continues. And the continued narrative of Acts 20 further underscores the integral relationship between "breaking of bread" and its provision as a social condition for didactic conversation. One finds in Acts 20:11: "Then he went upstairs again and broke bread and ate. After talking until daylight, he left" (NIV). "Breaking of bread" is mentioned again before the narrative describes Paul as speaking again. It is important, therefore, to note that Paul's speaking in Acts 20:7 was interrupted by an account of his healing of a man who fell to the ground from the third floor. The narrative describes Paul as re-creating social condition in which he could speak after he heals the man; the breaking of bread was a form of affirming his social authority to speak. The narrative-literary function, therefore, of the breaking of bread before Paul's resumption of speech is strategic. The narrative highlights the social value of breaking of bread.

Indeed, some texts portray breaking of bread as a value in itself. For instance, Acts 2:42 lists four things of value pursued by believers: "They devoted themselves to the apostles' teaching and to the fellowship, to the breaking of bread and to prayer" (NIV). This passage is part of the same narrative which describes breaking of bread as one of the factors in the increase of the number of believers. Acts 2:46-47 states: "Every day they continued to meet together in the temple courts. They broke bread in their homes and ate together with glad and sincere hearts, praising God and enjoying the favor of all the people. And the Lord added to their number daily those who were being saved" (NIV). One cannot deny the attributed value of the breaking of bread on the part of the narrator.

In the narrative accounts of Acts, breaking of bread functioned to create a social condition for the breaker of the bread to engage in didactic instruction and for the participants to gain a part of that social authority attributed to the breaker of the bread, the authoritative individual. Thus, it is not surprising that the symbols food and eating practice play a significant role in the portrayal of empowerment of gentiles in Acts 10 and 11.

Peter's vision in Acts 10:9-16 regarding God sanctioning eating of unclean animals finds interpretation in inclusion of gentiles into the social circle of the Jewish Christians. In the vision, Peter is told to kill and eat animals, which included both clean and unclean animals, "all kinds of four-footed animals, as well as reptiles of the earth and birds of the air" (v. 12 NIV). Peter objects, by claiming that nothing impure had entered his mouth (v. 14). A voice, understood to be from God, tells Peter, "Do not call anything impure that God has made clean" (v. 15 NIV). The text portrays Peter as not clearly understanding the meaning of the vision (v. 17). The meaning becomes clear only when gentile representatives of a gentile,[3]

---

[3]Howard Clark Kee speculates the possibility that Cornelius was depicted as a Jew in the narrative, but concludes finally that he was a gentile "drawn to the God of the Jews, one whose manner of life displays forms of Jewish religiosity: his personal piety (*eusebes*), his 'fearing God,' and his 'charitable contributions,' which seem to have been made to the wider society (*to lao*)" (To Every Nation under Heaven: The Acts of the Apostles (Harrisburg: Trinity Press International, 1997) 132-133).

named Cornelius, enter the narrative looking for Peter (vv. 17-18). The narrative describes the Spirit instructing Peter to go with the three men, the gentiles, who were looking for him, and not to "diakrinai". The presence of the narrative introduction, "While Peter was still thinking about the vision" in verse nineteen further underscores the relationship between the vision episode and the saying of the Spirit in verses nineteen and twenty.

The interpretation of the vision as a tool for empowerment of gentiles garner further support in the next narrative episode which finds setting in the house of Cornelius (vv. 24 ff.). The narrative portrays Peter as explaining the meaning of the vision in a speech to a gathering of people, composed of Cornelius' relatives and close friends (v. 24). The text attributes to the kerygma of Peter: "You are well aware that it is against our law for a Jew to associate with a Gentile or visit him. But God has shown me that I should not call any man impure or unclean" (v. 28). The reference to "impure" and "unclean" is clearly related to the unclean food of the vision, of which Peter was instructed to partake.

Narrative interest in the empowerment of gentiles is further accentuated in a complete reiteration in chapter eleven of Acts, in the context of Peter's report before the "circumcised believers" (v. 2). The narrative context is important. Peter is, in fact, answering charges that he went to the house of uncircumcised and ate with them (v. 3). The hostile environment further creates a narrative tension which highlights the significance not only of the vision but also of the recorded action that was interpretive of the vision. The narrative introduction in chapter eleven highlights the unacceptability of Peter's actions and casts Gentiles as the other with whom no association or meal fellowship should occur. The charge is significant in that Peter is not castigated for having baptized gentiles. It is the very act of social association that is criticized. This text portrays the gentile as the emblem of the other who is outside of the social referential. The gentile is the unclean, with whom one must not associate. Obvious analogy exists between the relationship between clean and unclean food on the one hand, and the circumcised (Jewish Christians) and the uncircumcised (gentiles) on the other. Relational value revolves not around baptism but around circumcision. Thus, those who are circumcised belong to the "in" group and can participate together in eating practices that empower, whereas the uncircumcised belong to the "out" group and, therefore, have no place in eating practices with members of the "in" group and in the corresponding empowerment.

It is this basic "in" group referential that the narrative works to undermine. Before the circumcised believers, Peter describes the vision and explains what follows. The vision is straightforward and basically corresponds to the original description in Acts 10. However, Peter's description of the following events, while corresponding to the narrative in Acts 10, accentuates interpretive elements in favor of social inclusion of gentiles as carrying implicit divine sanction. For instance, Peter explains: "As I began to speak, the Holy Spirit came on them as he had come on us at the beginning. Then I remembered what the Lord had said: 'John baptized with water, but you will be baptized with the Holy Spirit.' So if God gave them the same gift as he gave us, who believed in the Lord Jesus Christ, who was I to think that I could oppose God?" (vv. 15-17 NIV). In the literary form of a kerygma, Peter explains the justification for inclusion, and thereby empowerment, of the gentiles.

This is not surprising in light of the narrative intent not only of this textual unit, but also of the two previous textual units in chapter 10 – the vision pericope and the narrative episode set in the house of Cornelius. The intent is to show the empowerment of gentiles in the context in which such empowerment is not favorable. Various literary devices are utilized: (1) vision; (2) interpretation of vision; (3) divine sanction in the form of spirit (both verbal in reference to Peter and visual in reference to the gentiles); (4) approval of circumcised believers.

Innate to all three literary units in Acts 10-11 is the thematic understanding that there are exclusive foods and eating practices for the "in" group and that they are essential to empowerment. It is through the breaking down of the "in" group framework for social inclusion and the expansion of social referencing beyond the social value of circumcision that gentiles enter into eating practices that empower.

Contrary to Acts 10-11, which seem to point toward efforts to include gentiles into Jewish Christian circles, Acts 15 provides a picture into an effort to restrict the extent to which gentiles who became Christians could participate in Jewish Christian circles.

In Acts 15, one finds the account of a council in Jerusalem,[4] in which James makes a decision restricting gentile Christians from partaking certain foods. Acts 15:19-21 attributes to the ruling of James: "It is my judgment, therefore, that we should not make it difficult for the Gentiles who are turning to God. Instead we should write to them, telling them to abstain from food polluted by idols, from sexual immorality, from the meat of strangled animals and from blood. For Moses has been preached in every city from the earliest times and is read in the synagogues on every Sabbath" (NIV). It is important to note two arguments in the excerpt for outlining the food restriction: (1) the portrayal of food regulation as something that is not restrictive; (2) argument for food regulation based on purported long tradition of the message of Moses and on the continued teaching of it in the synagogue.

An obvious question rises: What is so important about these food regulations that they become representative of what gentile believers should observe? The answer is that these food regulations functioned to socially regulate empowerment

---

[4]David A. Fiensy argues that "The Jerusalem church, almost from the very beginning if not actually from Pentecost on, was culturally pluralistic. One cannot speak of an Aramaic stage followed by a hellenistic Jewish stage. These 'stages' were always contemporaneous. The two subcultures within the early church – the Aramaic and the Greek – were two springs flowing from the same source and in turn nourishing together the subsequent Gentile Christianity" ("The Composition of the Jerusalem Church," <u>The Book of Acts in Its Palestinian Setting</u>, ed. Richard Baukham [Grand Rapids: William B. Eerdmans Publishing Company, 1995, pp. 213-236] 235-236).

(or social inclusion) of gentile Christians. To fully understand the answer, one must consider the context in which one finds the decision attributed to James. The decision represents narrative conclusion to the question posed in the beginning of the literary unit, Acts 15:1-21. Acts 15:1 states: "Some men came down from Judaea to Antioch and were teaching the brothers: 'Unless you are circumcised, according to the custom taught by Moses you cannot be saved'" (NIV). The narrative describes Paul and Silas participating in dispute with the holders of this position, trying to maintain previous framework for social inclusion, such as participation in eating practices, in which circumcision was an important social referential. The dispute leads Paul and Silas to journeying as emissaries to Jerusalem to discuss this issue with apostles and elders.

Narrative repetition, and elaboration, of the issue appears in verse five of the same literary unit: "Then some of the believers who belonged to the party of the Pharisees stood up and said, 'The Gentiles must be circumcised and required to obey the law of Moses'" (NIV). The real issue, as repeated here, is maintaining previous social referential as the framework in which one is empowered. These proponents propose to create "fictive Jews" to maintain social referencing in the old framework of Jewish Christians participants in "in" group activities, includeing eating practices. The gentile must adopt Jewish characteristics and behavior to be accepted in the "in" group of Jewish Christians. Thus, this was a means to exert social control. The following verses present discussion of the issue in the gathering of apostles and elders.

It is interesting to note that the literary episodes from Acts 10 and 11 are repeated in a pithy kerygmatic form. The narrative attributes to the kerygma of Peter:

> God, who knows the heart, showed that he accepted them by giving the Holy Spirit to them, just as he did to us. He made no distinction between us and them, for he purified their hearts by faith. Now then, why do you try to test God by putting on the necks of the disciples a yoke that neither we nor our fathers have been able to bear? (Acts 15:8-10 NIV).

The narrative portrays in Peter an argument for shifting of previously primary referencing elements, such as circumcision or traditional observance, and of redefining the whole framework in which to participate in the in-group, such as eating practices. This idea found in Acts 15 is congruent with the conceptualization in the literary units found in Acts 10 and 11. The real issue is, indeed, empowerment of gentiles.

In light of the issue of empowerment, the decision attributed to James is telling. Traditional referencing, such as circumcision, is denigrated to a position of no importance for gentiles who become Christians. No other traditional laws require observance, except for four food regulations. Thus, the gentile believer becomes a part of a larger in-group framework of Jewish Christians that does not involve circumcision or many of the other traditional regulations that Jewish Christians were in the habit of observing. However, four food regulations moderate the empowerment of gentiles. Although gentiles participate in food and eating practices, they need to observe regulations that they did not need to observe as pagans, who readily consumed food sacrificed ritually in their previous social and religious context.

The concern of James and the Jerusalem leadership for this regulation of empowerment of gentile Christians in the narrative is further underscored in the multiple attestation of the regulation. The four food regulations are again attested inside the letter which the apostles and elders with the whole church (Acts 15:22), draft: "You are to abstain from food sacrificed to idols, from blood, from the meat of strangled animals and from sexual immorality. You will do well to avoid these things" (NIV).

This regulation is also attested in Acts 21:25, which finds itself within the narrative setting of Paul's arrival in Rome: "As for Gentile believers, we have written to them our decision that they should abstain from food sacrificed to idols, from blood, from the meat of strangled animals and from sexual immorality" (NIV). In the context of the narratives of Acts, this textual attestation seems redundant. Why does the text attribute to James and the elders a mention of this, when in fact chapter fifteen portrays that their decision was partially the result of the inquiry of Paul and Silas? Later in chapter fifteen, the letter is drafted by apostles and elders and the whole church with Paul's knowledge as verses twenty-two, a part of the narrative introduction to the writing of the letter, and verse twenty-five, a part of the drafted letter, indicate. Such unnecessary narrative repetition underscores the concern for moderation of gentile empowerment on the part of James and Jerusalem leadership.

Empowerment is the key concept associated with food and eating practices in Acts. In the social context of Jewish Christianity, Jesus granted social authority to his disciples, with whom he participated in eating practices. Peter as a representative recipient of that empowerment attempts successfully to bring gentiles into participation in empowering eating practices. James and the Jerusalem leadership influenced by kerygmae of Peter concur with the shift in the framework of social referencing and, therefore, do not engage in creating "fictive Jews" to fit into the previous framework, which required important Jewish symbols, such as circumcision, to be included in the in-group of the Jewish Christians.

Yet, James and the Jerusalem leadership were not interested in fully empowering gentile Christians. Thus, they tendered their empowerment by imposing regulations regarding food that was foreign to gentile Christians, although common to a Jewish Christian familiar with traditional Jewish practices. This picture of empowerment and power politics associated with food and eating practices in the narratives of Acts provides a view into their important function in early Christianity.

What serves as the model of significant breaking of bread narratives in the book of Acts? There are two possible models which may function to provide contextual precedent or reference point for understanding the function of food and "breaking of bread" in the book of Acts; namely, the Graeco-Roman symposium and the "open table fellowship" of Jesus of Nazareth. Upon closer examination of these two possible historical references, one comes to see that the open table fellowship of Jesus of Nazareth was more likely precedent for breaking bread narratives.

Greek symposion spans several centuries beginning as early as the fifth century Greece to beyond the period of the composition of the book of Acts. It functioned as a fellowship involving food and wine [5] around which various forms of entertainment, such as conversation, poetry reading, and sexual pleasure, revolved.[6] Although there is some variance in the Greek symposion of the fifth century and the Roman one of Late Antiquity, especially in terms of emphasis, the basic quality, or even philosophical outlook, of the symposion remained the same. An example of this is found in the topic of eros and pleasure of love being an integral part of the symposion. Ezio Pelizer writes:

---

[5]Michael Vickers states: "It might be as well to point out that the word *symposion* should, strictly speaking, only be applied to the serious drinking that occurred after the meal proper, the *deipnon*, was over..." (Greek Symposia [London, The Joint Association of Classical Teachers] 1).

[6]See various articles on the symposion, contained in Oswyn Murray (ed.), Sympotica: A Symposium on the *Symposion* (Oxford: Clarendon Press, 1990).

A ... fundamental element in the *symposion*, about which much remains to be said, is that of the amorous discourse which is developed in the course of it. *Eros* and the pleasures of love figure among the most characteristic subjects of the *logos sympotikos*, both in its poetic expression and in the eloquent philosophical discussion which was to typify the 'literary; *symposion* from Plato and Xenophon onwards.[7]

Symposion was a meal fellowship to indulge in literary and physical pleasure.

Entertainment,[8] that was so characteristic of the symposion, is certainly not the emphasis on passages involving breaking of bread in the book of Acts. As was shown, the breaking of bread functioned as a means of providing a sort of authority to the breaker of the bread and giving social power to the participants of the ritualized practice. The textual concern in the book of Acts is with social empowerment of gentiles and their inclusion into the authorized and

---

[7] "Outlines of a Morphology of Sympotic Entertainment," Sympotica: A Symposium on the *Symposion*, ed. Oswyn Murray (Oxford: Clarendon Press, 1990, pp. 177-184) 180.

[8] See various articles in Sympotica: A Symposium on the *Symposion* : Burkhard Fehr, "Entertainers at the Symposion: The *Akletoi* in the Archaic Period" (pp. 185-195); Annette Rathje, "The Adoption of the Homeric Banquet in Central Italy in the Orientalizing Period" (pp. 279-288); Nevio Zorzetti, "The *Camina Convivalia*" (pp. 289-307); and John D'Arms, "The Roman Convivium and the Idea of Equality" (pp. 308-320).

ritualized setting of the breaking of the bread. But the social concern of the author (or final redactor) of the book of Acts reaches far beyond the ritualized setting of the breaking of bread. The whole system of social exclusion comes into question.

Indeed, the narratives involving breaking of bread can be seen as propagandistic literature to champion social inclusion of gentiles into Jewish Christian circles. Jewish Christians portrayed in the book of Acts are involved in internal struggles regarding the place of the gentile in their social and religious system. This struggle comes further into focus in light of the passages involving the symbol and idea of food. Certain foods, considered sacred by Jewish Christians, lose their ritual import in the vision of Peter and in the narrative commentary. Furthermore, the textual description of the minimized observance requirement of food rules for gentiles – a decision by the Jerusalem Jewish Christian leadership – underscores the idea that the chief concern of the final redaction of the text is for the empowerment of gentiles. Breaking of bread (and food symbols) functions in the book of Acts to empower the breaker of the bread and the participant.

That is their chief function, and thus stands in contrast to the symposion, whose primary function was social preservation. In the symposion, the participants were select guests and of the educated elites. In other words, the symposion was a socially conservative mechanism to include those already inside the socially elite, and, thereby, exclude those outside of this social circle. Even the literature depicting this in the Greek and Latin corpus are elite literature; namely, literature that is produced by and consumed by the socially elite, primarily.

The seeming emphasis on the empowerment and inclusion of the gentiles into Jewish Christian circles leads us into the discussion of the open table fellowship of Jesus of Nazareth. By open table fellowship, we refer to the practices portrayed in the gospels, in which Jesus of Nazareth partakes of fellowship involving food with the socially disenfranchised of society. The texts frequently place in the mouth of the opponents of Jesus of Nazareth the accusation to this effect: "He eats with tax collectors and sinners."[9] Indeed, the narratives of gospels portray Jesus of Nazareth sharing food and associating with prostitutes, the ritually impure, and even gentiles, such as the Syro-Phoenician woman with a demon possessed daughter (Mark 7:24-30).

The logical question that presents itself then is: Is the open table fellowship of Jesus of Nazareth a historical precedent for the purpose of the breaking of bread (and the symbolic function of food) in the book of Acts? The answer is a qualified "yes."

The difficulty of seeing open table fellowship as a historical precedent for the portrayal of breaking of bread and food symbolism in the narratives of Acts relates to the question of determining historicity of an event or actual practice from texts that describe them. Should the reader reading the narratives in the gospels understand what is contained therein as an accurate portrayal of the events that transpired? Or is it to a certain extent a collective memory of a community that has experienced several generations of

---

[9]Mark 2:15-16; Matthew 9:10-11; Luke 5:29-30.

theological inquiry and symbolization of particular practices? The question, therefore, goes to the question of the Sitz im Leben of the practices and the narratives in the gospels.

It is possible that the open table fellowship could have partly served as a precedent for the concerns for inclusivity of gentiles in inner Jewish Christian circles in the book of Acts. Indeed, many scholars engaged in the quest for the historical Jesus [10] at the current time see Jesus' open table fellowship as belonging to the Sitz im Leben of Jesus of Nazareth. One such scholar is Gerhard Lohfink, who writes:

> It was characteristic of Jesus that he constantly *established community* – precisely for those who were denied community at that time, or who were judged inferior in respect to religion. Jesus made clear through his word and even more through his concrete conduct that he did not recognize

---

[10] For a survey of the quest for the historical Jesus, see W. Barnes Tatum, In Quest of Jesus: A Guidebook (Louisville: John Knox Press, 1982). Also, for a good discussion of a current leading criteria-theory in the quest for the historical Jesus, see chapter six of John P. Meier, A Marginal Jew: Rethinking the Historical Jesus (New York: Doubleday, 1991). There are other useful books that take open table fellowship of Jesus as a starting point for further historical analysis, such as found in John Dominic Crossan, The Historical Jesus: The Life of a Mediterranean Jewish Peasant (New York: HarperSanFrancisco, 1991).

religious-social exclusion and discrimination.[11]

Accepting this position would situate the practice of open table fellowship well before the breaking of bread narratives of Acts.

However, there is still the question of influence. Just because an event preceded an event or literature does not indicate influence. Yet, there is a likelihood that a practice that is situated in the Sitz im Leben of Jesus of Nazareth and transmitted[12] and preserved through several generations to the time of the composition of the book of Acts did have an influence on the purpose and content of practices, such as of breaking bread, in the book of Acts. From the standpoint of inclusivity, the open table fellowship of Jesus of Nazareth and the breaking of bread narratives in the book of Acts share congruence. And it is possible that Jesus of Nazareth's concerns

---

[11]Gerhard Lohfink, Jesus and Community (Philadelphia: Fortress Press, 1984) 88.

[12] Various scholars have written about the continued Jesus movement that embodied the open table fellowship of Jesus of Nazareth. One such scholar is Richard Horsley, who writes: "In reaction to the disintegration of local village communities and the decline of patriarchal authority, the Jesus movement apparently revitalized local life in terms of egalitarian non-patriarchal familial communities" (Sociology and the Jesus Movement [New York: Crossroad, 1989] 128). Another helpful analysis of the continued Jesus movement in light of the concept of open table fellowship is found in Gerd Theissen, Sociology of Early Christianity, trans. J. Bowden (Philadelphia: Fortress Press, 1978). Also, helpful is Bengt Holmberg, Sociology and the New Testament: An Appraisal (Minneapolis: Fortress Press, 1990).

for the social outcasts of his society could have functioned as a logical precedent for the inclusion of gentiles who were outside of the society in the mind of more forward thinking Christian Jews, represented in the narratives of Acts.

Thus, although from a literary standpoint, positing direct influence of open table fellowship on the breaking of bread narratives of Acts can be problematic, certain ideas of inclusivity can have functioned as an ideological model in the formation of the conceptual content of the breaking of bread narratives of the book of Acts. Relevant in this regard is the scholarly consensus that the gospel of Luke functions as a complementary literary unit with the book of Acts. Taken at face value, this would attribute the open table fellowship of Jesus of Nazareth in the gospel of Luke and the breaking of bread narratives in the book of Acts to the same author, which could more likely point to their literary congruence. In fact, Philip Francis Esler believes that such a table fellowship forms central unifying theme of the gospel of Luke and the book of Acts. Esler writes in a strong language:

> One issue in Luke-Acts towers above all others as significant for the emergence and subsequent sectarian identity of the type of community for whom Luke wrote: namely, table-fellowship between Jews and Gentiles. An almost universal failure to appreciate the centrality of this phenomenon, both to Luke's history of Christian

beginnings and to the life of his own community, is one of the most outstanding deficiencies in Lucan scholarship.[13]

Esler is interested in the coherence of Luke's ideology and does not necessarily argue that the praxis of Jesus of Nazareth in his Sitz im Leben was the influence of Luke's contemporary experience.

In terms of praxis, it may be more likely that the ideas of Paul were a greater immediate influence, if not the ideological precedent, for inclusion of gentiles into the Jewish Christian majority. Of course, open table fellowship and Pauline ideology do not have to be mutually exclusive in trying to assess influence on the breaking of bread narratives in the book of Acts.

Pauline texts, which some dated much earlier[14] than some gospel texts[15], may have functioned as a precedent for the breaking of bread passages in the book of Acts.[16] Breaking of bread in

---

[13] Philip Francis Esler, Community and Gospel in Luke-Acts: The Social and Political Motivations of Lucan Theology (Cambridge: Cambridge University Press, 1987) 71.

[14] For instance, Werner Georg Kümmel dates the composition of I Corinthians to 54/55 AD (Introduction to the New Testament, trans. Howard Clark Kee [Nashville: Abingdon Press, 1975] 279).

[15] Kümmel dates the composition of Luke between 70 to 90 AD (151).

[16] Regarding the dating of Acts, Kümmel writes: "Since Acts, as the second part of the Lukan double work, must have been written later than Lk, which was written after 70 ..., it could not have been produced before 80; the linguistic difference between Lk and Acts require a certain time lapse between the two

the Pauline corpus often take on theological and fictive-cultic significance – such as the idea that the breaking of bread symbolizes Jesus' body broken, or crucified, on the cross.[17] But the idea found in the Pauline corpus that Christianity is a property of gentiles as well and the idea that traditional rules that Jewish Christians observed were not ritually binding on gentiles[18] could have functioned as an ideological precedent for the textual concern of the inclusion of gentiles into Jewish Christian circles.

Perhaps, more helpful in understanding the breaking of bread narratives in the book of Acts is to

---

writings by the same author" (185-186). A side note to this quote of Kümmel is that it may be useful in light of linguistic differentiation to examine the gospel of Luke and the book of Acts as separate enterprise by different authors (or schools of authors).

[17] I Corinthians 11:17-24. Gerd Theissen argues that the picture provided here is that Paul's directive regarding the apparent ritual table fellowship was, in fact, a regular meal, that had participants from different socio-economic classes. Paul was trying to create a harmonious environment for all Christians participating in the communal meal. See chapter four of his book, The Social Setting of Pauline Christianity: Essays on Corinth (Philadelphia: Fotress Press, 1982).

[18] Galatians provides a picture into the concern of Paul on the inclusion of gentiles into Jewish Christianity without having to take up traditional Jewish observance. Thus, James D. G. Dunn writes: "Paul's concern was rather with he relation between Jew and Gentile. His question was not, How can I be saved?, but, How can Gentiles be included within the messianic community of Israel?" (Jesus, Paul and the Law: Studies in Mark and Galatians [Louisville: Westminster/John Knox Press, 1990] 130-131). Another useful work for understanding Paul's inclusivity ideology is E. P. Sander's book, Paul, the Law, and the Jewish People (Philadelphia: Fortress Press, 1983).

see it in contrast to other meta-ideas in the book of Acts. One significant symbol that seems to stand in opposition is the Temple. The Temple in Jerusalem is represented in the narratives of Acts as embodying the rules that Jewish Christians valued and used as an exclusionary tactic. Thus, in the book of Acts, Temple takes on a somewhat negative symbolization. John Elliot's discussion of the Temple versus household, the context in which breaking of bread was often performed, in his article "Temple Versus Household in Luke-Acts: A Contrast in Social Institutions"[19] is particularly helpful in understanding the value of the breaking of bread narratives in the book of Acts.

     John H. Elliot argues that the Temple functioned as a boundary marker. Temple was a place where sacrifice was offered and prayers were liturgically delivered. It was a public place of sanctity in which Israelites as a group of worshippers participated in reaffirming their belongingness. Temple necessitated social structures centered around the conceptualization of the holy. Thus, the priests were set apart as holy and these were the individuals who participated in leading the people in all things that are considered holy, such as sacrifices and prayers. The non-priestly participant's social place in the Temple was hierarchically inferior to that of the priest.[20]

---

[19] John H. Elliot, "Temple Versus Household in Luke-Acts: A Contrast in Social Institutions," The Social World of Luke-Acts: Models for Interpretation, ed. Jerome H. Neyrey (Peabody, MA: Hendrickson Publishers, Inc., 1991) pp. 211-240.
[20] Elliot 212-215

As was crucial to the maintenance of the holiness of the Temple, purity laws found emphasis and gained religious significance. But this religious significance was integrally tied to social significance. Observance of ritual purity was a restrictive social ordering that imputed value to an individual within the Temple-focused purity system.

John H. Elliott argues that the "household" stood in contrast to the Temple, in that it did not have a restrictive social system. For Elliott, the household represented all the qualities that were different from, even opposed to, the restricted Temple system – from a social perspective. But on the other hand, the Temple and the Household did not represent two opposing systems, but rather two differing and even complementing elements in the overall social system. John H. Elliott writes: "Like his ancient contemporaries, he spoke not of schematized wholes but rather of related parts: temple as a holy place of prayer and sacrifice, priests, rulers, Law and lawyers, purity observance; and household as homes, family members, servants, friends, meals, hospitality, and domestic life."[21]

Thus, to a certain extent the household represented an anti-type of the Temple. It was not necessarily a holy space in which all those pertaining to the understanding and practice of the holy were to be contained. Rather, the household, by the virtue of the fact that it included members who were not necessarily ritually pure nor even Israelite, provided an environment in which religious hierarchy centered around holiness was not the chief motivating factor

---

[21]Elliot 212. Emphasis his.

for social ordering. Rather social order centered around set of values that did not pertain to the holy – such as familial relationship, such as that between a father and son, or around master-slave relationship, or friendships. Of course, it may be extreme to say that religious social ordering did not have any influence on the social ordering of the household. However, by the very reality that the head of the household belonged to the class of people who would be considered "profane" in the religious hierarchy centered around the Temple, the nature of the household, in most cases, did not take on a religious character.

Seen in this light, the household stood as a contrast to what some considered as a restrictive religious system of the Temple. Luke, the supposed author of Acts, is one such figure. The Book of Acts portrays the Temple as a negative institution. For instance, Acts 6:13-14 portrays that Stephen was charged with speaking "word against this holy place and the law," for which he is described as having been stoned to death. Acts 21:26-36 (and Paul's defense in Acts 22-26) portrays Paul's temple visit resulting in a plot against his life. The negative characterization of the Temple in the book of Acts stands in contrast to the household, which exudes inclusivity and warmth.

It is, indeed, this inclusive household that functions as the primary setting, which the author of the book of Acts describes as being used as a medium of the Christian movement. John H. Elliott writes:

> In Acts the household becomes increasingly prominent as the scene and focus of the Christian movement which gradually shifts from Jerusalem and the temple to the households of the diaspora. At first the messianic community gathers both at the temple and in households (2:43-47; 5:42). But the attempt at peaceful coexistence fails. Agents of the temple become the hunters and followers of Jesus, the hunted. Stephen's speech and his stoning in connection with remarks concerning the temple form a turning point between the earliest phase of the church's life and its connection with the temple (Acts 1:1-8:1a) and its full-scale mission to households of the diaspora (8:1b-28:31).[22]

If, indeed, Elliott is correct in his assessment that the interest of the author(s) and the final redactor of the book of Acts is, at least in part, elevating the household over the Temple, then one sees how the breaking of bread, usually done in the context of the household in the book of Acts becomes strategic for advancing the ideology of including gentiles into the inner social circle of Jewish Christians. But one thing is clear – the Temple in the book of Acts receives, by in large, a negative characterization, whereas the household receives a positive portrayal.

---

[22] 216.

The household is, indeed, the place where the breaking of bread is often performed.

The narratives in Acts involving breaking of bread and food symbolism show strategic interest in elevating the social place of the gentile in Jewish Christianity. The breaker of the bread is empowered and often engages in didactic instruction and the participants in the breaking of bread practice receive empowerment. This setting in which gentiles receive empowerment is contrasted with the Temple, which the narrator of the book of Acts describes as restrictive and counter to that purpose.

From the standpoint of the breaking of bread narratives and their emphasis, the Temple functions as a literary device for providing a contrast and strengthening the propagandistic [23] agenda of the

---

[23] Martin Hengel defines the genre of Acts as a "historical monograph" (Acts and the History of Earliest Christianity [Philadelphia: Fortress Press, 1979] 36). Hengel defines "historical monograph" as "specialist histories on quite limited themes: individual provinces, cities, nations and sanctuaries, or even 'notable' features" (14). Although this genre definition is helpful for understanding the whole tenor of the narratives of Acts, it may be worthwhile to explore the intent of the narrative, which has intentionally propagandistic elements, in assessing the literary genre of the work. There have been considerations of considering the narratives of Acts as a political apologetic, to which Richard Cassidy rightly offers his objections (Society and Politics in the Acts of the Apostles [Maryknoll: Orbis Books, 1988, chapter 10]. I would take his criticism one step further by saying that it is not an apology, a form of defensive literature, at all, but rather a propagandistic literature, offensive in nature with a particular purpose in mind. As is garnered from the narratives studied in this paper, the propaganda was for the inclusion of gentile Christians in inner Jewish Christian circles.

narrator of the book of Acts. The Temple was counter-productive to the inclusion of gentiles into the community of followers of Jesus of Nazareth because it was difficult to divest of the temple cultic and ritual requirements. The household was the ideal place for gentile Christian empowerment because it was largely divested of the cultic focus attached to the Jerusalem Temple.

This propaganda is directed inwardly to the early Christian movement to which the author of the narratives belonged.

The Key Signifier of 'Forever' in Psalms of Solomon 11[1]

In Psalms of Solomon 11, the key signifier of "forever" is used to spur people toward traditional Jewish piety with the Jerusalem Temple and the temple cult as the focus. The poet systematically used the literary device at a time of great religious ambiguity on account of conflicting Jewish sectarian movements and in the context of deep social upheavals where traditional Jewish mores conflicted with the popularizing Hellenistic value system. The key signifier of "forever" was a meaningful and effective literary device and represents continuity with the past where עולם became identified with the covenant and the fulfilment of the covenant in the Jerusalem Temple.[2] It was this key signifier that the

---

[1] This paper was delivered in the Apocrypha and Pseudepigrapha Section of the 2005 International Meeting of the Society of Biblical Literature in Singapore (June 26 – July 1). I would like to thank Professor Jon Asgeirsson of the University of Iceland, who chaired the section and gave some helpful comments. I would also like to thank Professor Mark Harding of Australian College of Theology and Professor Rivka Nir of Open University of Israel for their helpful questions.

[2] Key signifier can be seen as an extension of (or building upon) what is generally referred to as biblical historiography. Thomas L. Thompson defines biblical historiography as "an intellectual tradition of morally and religiously critical commentary on Israel's past, reflected in the biblical texts. This intellectual tradition, most notably centering on themes of 'promise,' 'covenant,' and various forms of 'divine providence,' has been seen to inform a wide range of literature" (Thomas L.

poet of Psalms of Solomon 11 effectively used to encourage his readers towards temple-based piety and to prod Jewish religious reform. A key signifier is defined as a term or phrase that triggers a collective memory or a community value that is over-arching and all-encompassing. A key signifier functions aggressively in the literary context to spur audience to action. In the context of apocryphal literature, generally the action sought is a deeper religious devotion. In the specific case of Psalms of Solomon 11, the poet uses the key signifier of "forever" to elicit devotion to the redemptive value of the covenant and to solicit deeper religious devotion to traditional, temple-based Jewish piety.

The poet of Psalms of Solomon 11 was writing at a time of poignant sectarian conflicts within Judaism. Three main sects were the Pharisees, Sadducees, and the Essenes.[3] The Pharisees[4] were chiefly concerned with being faithful in the

---

Thompson, *Early History of the Israelite People: From the Written and Archaeological Sources* <Leiden: E. J. Brill, 1994>, p. 375).

[3] Emil Bock describes Pharisees, Sadducees, and the Essenes as exclusive in membership. Bock writes: "We are dealing with strict, segregated Orders, as is clear even from the writings of Josephus. An ordinary citizen could be a follower but not easily a member of one of these exclusive leading groups. Only a detailed consideration of the sternly esoteric character of these communities makes it possible to understand the historical role they played at the approach of the turning point of time" (Emil Bock, *Caesars and Apostles: Hellenism, Rome and Judaism* <Edinburgh: Floris Books, 1998>, p. 123).

[4] Emil Brock identifies Hasidim ("the Pious") in the book of Maccabees with the Pharisees (Bock, *Caesars and Apostles*, p. 63).

observance of the law[5] and focused their religiosity around the synagogue. The strength of their movement was in presenting themselves as faithful to the law as found in the Old Testament. Furthermore, the Pharisees are often seen as more parochially Jewish.

However, the Pharisees tended toward foreign influences, although appearing intentionally anti-foreign more often than not.[6] Emil Schürer argues: "But it is in effect only the garb that is borrowed from Greece. The substance itself is authentically Jewish."[7] Although the Pharisees participated in temple-based religious practices, their piety was often detached from the temple cult. This could have been partly due to their conflict with the Sadducees.[8] The majority of the leadership of the Pharisees was non-priestly. Thus, even though Rabbinic materials seem to elevate the Jerusalem Temple, it is important to note that the Pharisees were only one sect of Judaism and to be cautious about using Rabbinic materials to

---

[5] *B.J.* ii 8, 14 (162); *Vita* 38 (191); *Ant.* Xvii 2, 4 (41). Cf. Matthew 9:14; Luke 5:33; Matthew 23:25; Luke 11:39; Luke 11:42.

[6] In origin, the Pharisees were opposed to foreign influence. However, while maintaining Jewish identity, synagogues often functioned as receptacles of Hellenistic influence (Bock, *Caesars and Apostles*, pp. 124-125).

[7] Emil Schürer, *The History of the Jewish People in the Age of Jesus Christ (175 B.C.-A.D. 135): Volume II*, rev. and ed. Geza Vermes, Fergus Millar, and Matthew Black (Edinburgh: T. & T. Clark, 1979), p. 393.

[8] Both the New Testament and Josephus show the Pharisees and the Sadducees in conflict.

understand Judaism before the destruction of the Jerusalem Temple in 70 AD.[9] Emil Bock warns:

> When one tries, based on the Talmud, to form some ideas about the spiritual nature of Judaism during the last pre-Christian and first Christian century, one arrives at the completely erroneous one-sided notion that, even then, the Pharisaic stream was the only leading and dominant one.[10]

The portions in the Rabbinic literature elevating the Jerusalem Temple can be seen as written when the Jerusalem Temple ceased to exist and the inheritors of the Pharisaic movement no longer felt the threat from the Jerusalem Temple and its priestly leadership. During the Late Second Temple period, the Pharisees were in conflict with the Sadducees and their temple-based authority.

The Sadducees were more interested in the temple cult and a religiosity based on the temple. The Sadducees discouraged over-emphasis of the law and did not make rigid requirements for observance of the law as the Pharisees did. Furthermore, the Sadducees tended to be more openly friendly towards foreigners and foreign influences. The Sadducees represented the establishment. Emil Schürer des-

---

[9] Emil Schürer explains: "As in its attitude towards biblical law, so in its religious and doctrinal views Pharisaism essentially represented the standpoint of later rabbinic Judaism" (Schürer, *The History of the Jewish People: Volume II*, p. 391).
[10] Bock, *Caesars and Apostles*, p. 120.

cribes the Sadducees as "priests and their aristocratic lay allies who ruled the Jewish state"[11] since Persian times. As the Jewish state was under the authority of larger empires, the aristocracy – namely, the Sadducees – felt the need to court their favor. Emil Schürer describes the Sadducean socio-political reality:

> Whoever wished to achieve something politically in the world of that time had to be on a more or less friendly footing with Hellenism. So Hellenism gained increasing ground even among the leading priests in Jerusalem. And in a corresponding measure the latter became estranged from Jewish religious interests.[12]

Jewish religious interest to which Schürer refers to is of the traditional kind based on Torah. But despite their courtship of foreign influences and foreign powers, the Sadducees were Jewish aristocrats and their aristocratic power derived from the Jerusalem Temple. Thus, out of all the sectarian groups, the Sadducees had the greatest vested interest with the thriving of the Jerusalem Temple.

In principle, the Essenes believed in the Jerusalem Temple cult.[13] However, in practice they

---

[11] Schürer, *The History of the Jewish People: Volume II*, p. 404.
[12] Schürer, *The History of the Jewish People: Volume II*, p. 412.
[13] Josephus points out that the Essenes sent in their offerings to the Jerusalem Temple (*Ant.* Xviii 1, 5 (19). Cf. 1QS 9:3-5; CD 6:11-20; 11:17-21; 16:13).

distanced themselves from Jerusalem and the temple cult in Jerusalem. Under the leadership of the Teacher of Righteousness,[14] the Essenes sought to relocate themselves permanently in the desert.[15] It is thought to be at least in part due to violent conflicts with the Jerusalem Temple establishment. The Wicked Priest[16] figures prominently in the writings of the Essene community.

Similar to the Pharisees,[17] the Essenes emphasized the law.[18] However, Essenes tended to be more extreme in their legal observance. This is particularly evident in their Sabbath Day observance.[19] Like the Pharisees, Essenes tended to be outwardly anti-foreign. However, the Essenes were more extreme than the Pharisees and were meticulous in guarding against any foreign influence. And Essenes actively condemned Jews who compromised

---

[14] CD 1:10-11; 4QpPs 37ii 19, iii 15.

[15] Emil Schürer likens the Essenes to "a monastic order" (Schürer, *The History of the Jewish People: Volume II*, p. 558). George Wesley Buchanan agrees (George Wesley Buchanan, *The Consequences of the Covenant* <Leiden: E. J. Brill, 1970>, p. 242).

[16] Emil Schürer identifies the Wicked Priest as Jonathan who became the high priest in 153/2 B.C. (Schürer, *The History of the Jewish People: Volume II*, p. 587).

[17] Emil Schürer states that the Essenes, like the Pharisees, came from the Hasidim of the Maccabean period and they were led by "sons of Zadok" opposed to the Hasmonean dynasty (Schürer, *The History of the Jewish People: Volume II*, p. 413).

[18] Philo, *Quod omnis probus* 12 (80).

[19] *B.J.* II (147). Josephus notes that the Essenes were the most extreme of all Jews in Sabbath Day observance. Essenes prepared food the day before, refused to light a fire, and discouraged defecating on the Sabbath.

the Torah as the result of foreign influences. In fact, the Essene community stated that they were the true Israel and that when the messiah comes, he would destroy Jews who have compromised along with Gentiles. Then, the messianic kingdom would be established with them along with other righteous Jewish observers of the law. The Jerusalem Temple cult will be established in a proper way.

It is clear to see the extent of the sectarian conflict. The Essenes were, in a sense, wishing death upon the Pharisees and the Sadducees. The Pharisees and the Sadducees actually engaged in a conflict that turned bloody.[20] Jewish sectarian conflicts were spiralling out of hand. The poet of Psalms of Solomon can be seen as a reformer who was advocating reforming the current situation and returning to a more traditional piety and a focused temple-based religiosity of the past. It was a type of effort toward centralization of Judaism, and therefore can be seen as an attack on sectarianism.

Besides the great religious ambiguity due to proliferation of sectarian movements, the times witnessed social upheavals where traditional Jewish

---

[20] Josephus, *Ant.* xii (379-382); *Ant.* xiii 13, 5 (372-3); *B.J.* I 4, 3 (88). Alexander Jannaeus killing 800 Pharisees is seen as related to the conflict between the Pharisees (the lay law experts) and the Sadducees (those who were tied to the priestly aristocracy). In the Talmud, bSukk. 48b is understood as reflecting on the incident involving Alexander Jannaeus. A Sadducees poured libation of water on his feet instead of the altar, like he was supposed to. The response was that he was pelted with lemons by those opposed to the Sadducees. See C. Rabin, "Alexander Jannaeus and the Pharisees," *Journal of Jewish Studies* 7 (1956), pp. 3-11.

mores conflicted with the popularizing Hellenistic value systems. The extent of Hellenistic influence on Jews in Palestine is clear when we examine the texts. The Maccabean Revolt was preceded by a series of Jerusalem Temple high priests hackling with Hellenistic authorities for more money in return for pro-Hellenistic policies. Those pro-Hellenistic factions who catered to Hellenistic powers sought to Hellenize the Jewish populace in Palestine using their official positions – even that of the office of the High Priest – in the Jerusalem Temple. It is not difficult to see that if the highest official religious authority was susceptible to Hellenistic influences and even spread Hellenism, then religious leaders lower down in the Jerusalem Temple hierarchy were likely to be Hellenized as well. Sectarian movements had their fuel from the pervasiveness of Hellenism among Jewish religious leaders.

What were the ordinary people to do in a state of social confusion? There were those who joined more revolutionary groups like Sicarii who went around assassinating foreign officials and Jewish leaders who actively supported foreign influences. Others joined less violent religious sectarian movements.

The poet of Psalms of Solomon 11 looked towards another method. He sought to encourage religious reforms and go back to traditional, temple-based religiosity. Going back to traditional religiosity meant opposing Hellenistic influences. In a sense, it can be seen as reformist effort in light of what was happening among religious leaders, including the High Priest, in the establishment. In a sense, it was indirectly warning them against Hellenization.

Emphasizing a temple-focused religiosity can also be seen as reformist. The poet found sectarian religiosity as problematic in the midst of corruption and self-defeating inter-denominational conflicts. The poet realized that temple-focused religiosity will unite the Jews and strengthen Judaism. In fact, since the time of Ezra and Nehemiah, the Torah was seen as the absolute rule for religious observance and a primary dictate of the Torah was that only those of the line of Aaron could lead sacrifice. There was a growing non-priestly scribal force rising particularly around the time of the Maccabees, but they could not replace Temple priests as religious leaders according to Torah.[21] The poet of the Psalms of Solomon was interested in upholding the principle of the Torah regarding Temple worship.

It is important to note that the reform called for by the poet, therefore, involved two aspects: (1) traditional (ie., more parochially Jewish) direction and (2) temple-based (ie., centralizing) emphasis.

To encourage the two-sided reform, the poet of Psalms of Solomon 11 used the literary tool of key signifier. The key signifier that he used was the word "forever." As a key signifier, "forever" triggered the Jewish collective memory and prompted Jewish readers toward action – to move towards a traditional, temple-based piety.

How is "forever" a key signifier in Psalms of Solomon 11? To understand this phenomenon, it is necessary to review the history of the term "forever."

---

[21] Schürer, *The History of the Jewish People: Volume II*, p. 239.

"Forever" (in Hebrew, עולם) became a key signifier hundreds of years before the Psalms of Solomon's composition. Thus, by the time that the poet of Psalms of Solomon used the key signifier, it was a powerful literary device.

עולם was first used in a significant literary way in relation to the covenant,[22] as attested in Genesis 17.[23] The covenant made with God was an everlasting covenant. In a sense, therefore, עולם became the seal of the covenant with God or a way of signing the covenant with God. The covenant made with God was by nature an everlasting covenant. It points to the eternal nature of God (Psalms 93:2; Isaiah 46:10-11; Isaiah 63:16). It is impossible to make an everlasting covenant with other humans because humans are finite and die. עולם, therefore, became a covenant seal for the covenant made with God.

---

[22] G. Garbini states that the received Abraham tradition reflects the sixth-century Babylonian exile (G. Garbini, *History and Ideology in Ancient Israel* <London: 1988>, pp. 76-86. See also, J. van Seters, *Abraham in History and Tradition* (New Haven: 1975) and Thomas L. Thompson, *The Historicity of the Patriarchal Narratives* (BZAW 133) (Berlin: Walter De Gruyter, 1974). Even if we date the received covenant tradition to the sixth-century B.C., it would have been in place for hundreds of years and growing in influence via literary traditions by the time of the Psalms of Solomon.

[23] Thomas L. Thompson sees "Genesis 17 as a pivotal and interpretive narrative in the 'biography' of Abraham" (Thomas L. Thompson, *Early History of the Israelite People: From the Written and Archaeological Sources* <Leiden: E. J. Brill, 1994>, p. 358). Its placement was strategic in the context of the Abrahamic narrative.

Genesis 17 indicates the use of עולם as a covenant seal. Each of the four main stipulations of the covenant are signed, or sealed, with עולם (Genesis 17:7, 8, 13, 19). This, in effect, emphasizes that the nature of the covenant was a covenant with God. The force of עולם as a covenantal seal was felt in the corpus of Old Testament literature (Exodus 31:16-17; Leviticus 24:8; Numbers 18:19; 2 Samuel 23:5; Isaiah 55:3; Isaiah 61:8; Jeremiah 50:5; Ezekiel 16:60).

Whenever the covenant was invoked, it was remembered as an everlasting covenant (I Chronicles 16:14-18; Psalms 105:7-11; Psalms 111:5; Jeremiah 32:37-41). Thus, it is not surprising to find literary manifestation of demand for covenantal fulfilment in the Old Testament literature. God had promised the land to Abraham and this was an everlasting covenant, therefore it was understood that God was obliged to this covenant (Judges 2:1). The covenant seal of עולם was invoked.

The flip-side to invoking the covenant seal of עולם and claiming that God needed to bring Jews to Jerusalem was the claim that the Jews were obliged forever to keep their part of the covenant as descendants of Abraham. It is quite common to find in the Old Testament literature that the people were to observe their part of the covenant as a people or suffer punishment from God for breaking their part in the covenant (Psalms 78:9-22; Isaiah 24:5-6).

In fact, the Old Testament not only contains warnings against breaking the covenant, but it also contains justification for the exile and Jewish deaths at the hands of foreign armies as the result of breaking the covenant (Ezra 9:6-7; Nehemiah 9:32-35; Daniel 9:4-14). The key signifier of עולם required obligation to the covenant by the descendants of Abraham forever (Ezekiel 37:24-28). Keeping of the covenant would bind God to blessing and breaking the covenant would result in God's horrific punishment. And this would be for all time.

It is not difficult to see how "forever" functioned as a key signifier in the Old Testament. עולם called Israelites to action. The very mention of the key signifier demanded of Israelites to keep their part in the covenant, in other words, in proper cultic observance.

God promised land to Abraham and his descendants so that they could come and worship him in Jerusalem. Thus, giving of Jerusalem obligated Jews to worship God in Jerusalem. The idea is that God of the Jews dwells in Jerusalem (Psalms 132:11-18) when Jerusalem is given to Jews; thus, Jews must worship in Jerusalem. The worship of God must follow cultic rules and regulations.

The Exodus tradition[24] in the Old Testament further endorses the concept of cultic obligations on the part of the Jews (Nehemiah 9). God of Abraham brought the descendants of Abraham out of the land of Egypt and brought them into Jerusalem so that they would worship God properly in Jerusalem,

---

[24] Roland de Vaux writes: "In the Pentateuch in its present form, the story of the patriarchs is linked to the stories of the Exodus and the conquest of the Promised Land by the theme of the promise" (Roland de Vaux, *The Early History of Israel: To the Exodus and the Covenant of Sinai*, trans. David Smith <London: Darton, Longman & Todd, 1978>, p. 166).

God's dwelling place. The whole point of bringing the Israelites into Jerusalem was for proper cultic worship. Moses tells Pharaoh, "Let my people go so that they may worship me" (Exodus 8:1; Exodus 10:3). In a sense, therefore, God gives Israelites land of their own in order that they could fulfil their covenantal obligation in his dwelling place.

The Exodus tradition supports the key signifier of עולם's function to compel Israelites toward covenantal observance in practicing cultic requirements. In a sense, the covenant and the exodus become intertwined and integrally linked (Nehemiah 9). The exodus represents God's fulfilment of the covenant and God's demand that Israelites keep their part of the covenant.[25] The covenant was an everlasting covenant, or ברית עולם.

עולם, therefore, functioned as a key signifier to prompt Israelites to remember the covenant and spur them to action in cultic observance. This is an established literary tradition in the Old Testament literature. Israelites who were exposed to the Old

---

[25] It is important to note Thomas L. Thompson's comments about the impact of literary understanding of a reality or vision. Thompson writes: "It is not relevant whether that vision is historically accurate. It is not even essential that we affirm the historicity of a contemporary existent 'Israel' other than as a literary process in history through which this vision is achieved. The text presents us with a window into the intellectual world of the authors and tridents of the tradition's history, and enable us to understand how they understood their past" (Thompson, *Early History of the Israelite People*, p. 126). The received traditions of Exodus and the Abrahamic covenant testify to the understanding of the past. On the literary level, these two traditions had a lasting influence. The Psalms of Solomon can be seen as a beneficiary of that influence.

Testament literature understood the significance of the key signifier of עולם. And the key signifier of עולם continued to enjoy its import in the Old Testament literature and came to be integrated into the culture of those exposed to it for generations.

By the time of the poet of Psalms of Solomon 11 and his audience, "forever" was crystallized as a key signifier of great import in Jewish literature. Both the poet and his audience understood the significance of the key signifier of "forever." Both of them understood what was demanded of them.

The poet of Psalms of Solomon 11 expertly uses the key signifier of "forever" to trigger a collective memory and spur his audience to traditional temple-based religiosity. When we look at the attestation of forever in Psalms of Solomon 11 itself, this becomes even clearer.

The key signifier of "forever" (αἰῶνα) is found in Psalms of Solomon 11:9. In a sense, "forever" signs Psalms of Solomon 11 like the covenantal seal of "forever" (עולם) in Genesis 17. Psalms of Solomon 11:9 emphasizes God's part in the covenant. Just as God promised the land, he has given Jews the land by ingathering Jews to the land.

We see that "forever" is used strategically as a key signifier to invoke the collective memory of the covenant when we look at Psalms of Solomon 11. Verses 3-7 evoke a type of exodus account of God leading Jews and ingathering Jews to Jerusalem. The emphasis is that God himself brought them to Jerusalem (PssSol 11:2, 4). Furthermore, it is God who performed miracles – like flattening high mountains (PssSol 11:6, 7).

The commingling of the covenant with the exodus is not surprising given that this is an established literary practice. The Old Testament literature exhibits combining covenantal and exodus elements (Nehemiah 9). It is natural since the major literary event of exodus represents God's keeping of his part of the covenant, which is an everlasting covenant (ברית עולם). This tradition has been in effect for hundreds of years before the poet's time. In a similar way, "forever" has gained an important literary function – as a key signifier on a cultural level.

The poet of the Psalms of Solomon effectively tapped into this cultural and literary reality. The poet efficiently used the key signifier of "forever" along with covenant and exodus ideas associated with it. The poet emphasized with "forever" the idea that God has kept his covenant. As a key signifier, "forever," therefore, elicited collective memory and encouraged the readers toward action – which in this case was traditional, temple-based cultic observance. Psalms of Solomon 11:1 indicates trumpet-blowing for proper temple-based cultic worship. Psalms of Solomon 11:8 signals priests to wear their cultic vestments for proper temple sacrifice. The idea is clear that because God has kept his covenant in bringing Jews to Jerusalem, Jews were required to do their part in keeping the covenant. For the poet, this meant proper cultic worship at the Jerusalem Temple.

Bibliography

Bock, Emil. *Caesars and Apostles: Hellenism, Rome and Judaism.* Translated by Maria St. Goar. Edinburgh: Floris Books, 1998.

Buchanan, George Wesley. *The Consequences of the Covenant.* Leiden: E. J. Brill, 1970.

De Vaux, Roland. *The Early History of Israel: To the Exodus and Covenant of Sinai.* Translated by David Smith. London: Darton, Longman & Todd, 1978.

Garbini, G. *History and Ideology in Ancient Israel.* London: 1988.

Rabin, C. "Alexaner Jannaeus and the Pharisees." *Journal of Jewish Studies* 7 (1956), pp. 3-11.

Schürer, Emil. *The History of the Jewish People in the Age of Jesus Christ (175 B.C.-A.D. 135): Volume II.* Revised and edited by Geza Vermes, Fergus Millar, and Matthew Black. Edinburgh: T. & T. Clark, 1979.

Thompson, Thomas L. *Early History of the Israelite People: From the Written and Archaeological Sources.* Leiden: E. J. Brill, 1994.

Thompson, Thomas L. *The Historicity of the Patriarchal Narratives*. BZAW 133. Berlin: Walter De Gruyter, 1974.

Van Seters, J. *Abraham in History and Tradition*. New Haven: 1975.

About the Author

Heerak Christian Kim received his B.A. *cum laude* in history with a minor in classical studies from the University of Pennsylvania in Philadelphia. Kim received his M.A. in history in 1991 at the University of California, Los Angeles (UCLA) in the context of the Ph.D. program in the History Department. Kim pursued his theological training part-time while being a full-time student at UCLA and obtained his MA in Theology from Fuller Seminary in Pasadena.

Kim has conducted doctoral level research at the Hebrew University of Jerusalem, Harvard University, Brown University, and the University of Heidelberg in Germany. Currently, Kim is a Ph.D. candidate in Hebrew, Jewish, and Early Christian Studies at the University of Cambridge in the United Kingdom and resident at Jesus College, Cambridge.

Kim has received many prestigious fellowships and scholarships during the course of his research, such as the Lady Davis Fellowship and the Raoul Wallenberg Scholarship. Kim has taught undergraduate students at UCLA and Brown University. In Cambridge, Two separate committees (the New Testament Committee and the Old Testament Committee) have appointed him as a supervisor of undergraduate students at the University of Cambridge to teach courses in Hebrew, Jewish, and Early Christian Studies.

Currently, Heerak Christian Kim is particularly interested in methodological questions regarding the study of Biblical texts and ancient history. His ongoing research projects also include examining Jewish Law in the context of legal history and in comparison to modern legal systems, an interest sparked while studying the Talmud with Professor Isaiah Gafni when he was a visiting professor at Harvard University in 1999.

Heerak Christian Kim is the author of *Hebrew, Jewish and Early Christian Studies: Academic Essays.*

www.ingramcontent.com/pod-product-compliance
Lightning Source LLC
Chambersburg PA
CBHW031138160426
43193CB00008B/186